ADDER

ROE BUCK.

SAND LIZARD

VICKY RESTING

Best wishes
to
June and Norman

Coleman

Monica

Monica Coleman's New Forest

With additional text
by ANNE RUFFELL
who also edited the book

Published by:
PAUL CAVE PUBLICATIONS
74 Bedford Place
Southampton

Printed by:
BROWN & SON (RINGWOOD) LTD
Crowe Arch Lane
Ringwood
Hampshire

First Published 1987
ISBN 0-86146-064-2

Colour Photography by:
PAUL S. PENROSE

Black and White Photography by:
ANNE RUFFELL

Colour reproduction by:
Aero Offset (Bournemouth) Ltd.

Black and white reproduction by:
Monochrome Scanning Ltd.

This book printed on Highland Supermatt paper, supplied by:
James McNaughton Paper Merchants Ltd.

Foreword

To many, the New Forest is a pleasant area to visit for a Sunday drive, or a picnic; to Monica Coleman it is the life-blood which flows through her veins and is the inspiration in her fingers. This is what makes her book about the New Forest different from any others. You are seeing the Forest through the eyes of a person who understands the ever-changing colours and textures which go to make up the character of this small island of beauty in Southern England. Through the gift of Monica's artistry on canvas and in words, you are able to share with her a romance.

Millions of visitors are attracted to this unique area but it is a fact that the average person who ventures into the Forest knows little of the real life dramas enacted every day in this sometimes hostile environment, perhaps only a few feet away from the hustle and bustle of the ever-encroaching spread of civilisation. In this book you will find the secrets of the Forest unfold before you.

Of the four seasons in the Forest, spring and autumn must be the two which present the artist with the most sensational material nature can offer. After a hard winter you can almost hear the awakening of the old woodlands as oak and beech burst forth into life and the forest floor becomes covered in a wealth of spring flowers. Spring is also the time when the miracle of life can be seen in the animal population. Leggy foals are born out of mares who have struggled for survival through the previous winter, their shaggy coats little protection against the biting winds which have taken their toll of the less hardy. Those elusive creatures, the deer, come together in large herds as if to rejoice in the coming of warmer weather. They exchange their drab winter coats and take on the 'Bambi' image as they eagerly await the arrival of their next generation.

At the onset of autumn, the Forest is turned into a wonderland of colour. Animals prepare for winter hibernation as they scamper about the crisp forest undergrowth looking for their share of the yearly harvest of nuts and fruits. Autumn also sees the start of the deer hunting season and one has to mention that because of Monica's love for the wildlife, she is determined to see an end to this outdated and cruel form of recreation.

I first met Monica, appropriately enough, in the heart of the Forest at an open-air meeting to launch the New Forest Deer Protection Council. Since that occasion in 1985, I have come to admire Monica both for her artistic skill and for her love and knowledge of the Forest flora and fauna. I shall be forever indebted to her for my first sighting of that noble beast, the Red Deer. It was because of her unerring instinct to know where deer can be seen in the Forest, that on a bright spring morning I found myself surrounded by these truly magnificent animals. These deer, once the quarry of royalty, are no longer prolific in the New Forest and are rarely seen by the casual visitor.

The Forest is a huge outdoor studio for Monica. Words alone cannot describe the extravaganza as each season passes, yet Monica is able to paint a true reproduction as a record for others to enjoy. She is truly a friend of the Forest and by being able to convey her feelings about it and its wildlife in both pictures and words, is helping to safeguard its future for generations to come.

Graham Sirl,
Chairman,
New Forest Deer Protection Council.

TO THE MEMORY OF

MY PARENTS

GEORGE AND LILIAN COLEMAN

THE CHALET DOWN
BY THE RIVER AT
"RIVERBEND."

CONTENTS

COLOUR PLATES

BLACK & WHITE HALF-TONES

Introduction

It was in April 1981 that I first heard of Monica Coleman when I watched B.B.C's television series 'The New Foresters'. Monica was featured painting a scene in the New Forest and the camera recorded the magic transformation of a bare canvas to finished work. I had lived on the edge of the New Forest for some years and although I had often taken photographs there, none seemed to capture the essence of the Forest like this painting. So attractive was it, I made a mental note to track down the artist one day.

Three years passed and I thought no more about it until one weekend when I chanced to be wandering through Ringwood with my husband. There in a bookshop window was a small painting which stopped me in my tracks. It depicted a leafy glade of white-barked trees reflected in a pool of water so real I felt if I could only touch it my finger would come away wet. With such subtle colouring and tranquil atmosphere, it was unmistakably the New Forest and the Artist was Monica Coleman.

As we stood admiring the painting, a young couple joined us. "We've just been to her studio," they said. "It's only around the corner near the recreation centre. She's having an open day and she gives all her visitors a free cup of tea." We were thirsty so we decided to go. It turned out to be the most expensive 'free' cup of tea we've ever had because I bought the picture! But it introduced me to Monica and that was the beginning of what was to become first a professional association — when I wrote a profile on her for 'Hampshire' magazine — and, later, friendship as we worked on this book together over the past three years.

In the time since we met, I have seen for myself at exhibitions the pleasure Monica's paintings give countless people. Sometimes I have witnessed people becoming so emotional as they view her work they can hardly speak. She touches a chord in them rather like the thrill experienced when listening to an uplifting piece of classical music or hearing a choirboy sing in St. Paul's Cathedral. By some strange osmotic process Monica's deep love of the Forest is conveyed and it is this intangible communication between artist and viewer that makes her work so special. Trying to define such a communication is impossible but many times I have heard people say "She's the only person who can paint the New Forest as it really is."

Monica always attends her exhibitions and people are delighted when they meet her. She is a down-to-earth type of woman who dresses comfortably in trousers, avoids the use of make-up, and has a friendly easy manner that instantly puts people at their ease. Her strong voice has a rich Hampshire accent and she has a keen sense of humour. Laughter frequently fills the gallery as she relates a story but sometimes she is self-conscious of smiling, having lost a front tooth at the age of twelve.

Since the showing of the television programme, Monica has become a local celebrity but fame has not changed her common-sense attitude to life. Now able to earn her living doing the one thing she really enjoys — painting the New Forest — she still gives thanks for the stroke of luck which placed her on television and gave her the opportunity to turn a hobby into a career, albeit a late one.

Monica does not profess to be an authority on the New Forest, nor is she a zoologist, botanist, entymologist or biologist. She is, to use her own description, an ordinary person with an enquiring mind who wants to learn all she can about the place from which she has gained so much.

The text of this book records some of the experiences Monica has had in the New Forest. She shares her joys and sorrows — there is beauty, peace, excitement, laughter and occasionally despair, anger and even ugliness. It is all part of a passionate love which has shaped and fulfilled one person's life and is a very personal view of a very public place — it is the special world of Monica Coleman's New Forest.

May 1987   *Anne Ruffell*

Monica and Sika at Woodford Bottom watching deer.

PART I

Glimpses into
Monica Coleman's Life

Monica Coleman's love affair with the New Forest began just over twelve years ago. It was then she went into the Forest for the first time with a few tubes of oil paints, a knife and a piece of hardboard. She sat in a sun-dappled clearing and painted the scene before her — leafy beech trees dipping their branches into a mirror-still pool. The resulting picture was a far cry from those she creates today but something happened as she painted.

"I felt as though a spell was being cast over me and as the picture took shape, so my excitement increased. I had been in the Forest hundreds of times before but never looked at it with the eye of an artist. Suddenly, a whole new world was opening up before me. As soon as I had finished the picture I wanted to do another . . . and another . . . and another. That special feeling has never left me."

At first Monica painted well-known beauty spots like Moyles Court, Rhinefield and Linford Bottom but as her passion for the Forest increased, so she delved deeper into its heart. Her knowledge of the life of the Forest — its shy creatures, plants, flowers, birds, insects — grows as she studies them first hand. With a keen eye for observation, she has an intimate knowledge of many areas and is continually spurred on to see and understand more.

Life for Monica revolves around the Forest and barely a day passes when she is not walking or painting there. The advent of each season brings her fresh delights and she finds it impossible to choose the time she loves best.

"When the leaves begin to turn I swear that autumn is my favourite season. There is nothing more beautiful than to paint in a glade with golden leaves falling all around you. But when the fresh pale green of spring begins to show after the long months

of winter, or when the sun fills the woods with patterns of light and shade, I realise I love those times too."

For the past six years Monica has been a full-time artist, able to get out into the Forest all through the year. Even in winter she will be seen tramping through the snow with her easel and paints, her fingers so numb with cold she can hardly hold the knife. To be able to spend so much time in the Forest gives her such happiness that she still sometimes pinches herself to make sure she is not dreaming.

The turning point in Monica's life came when she was featured on television in Dennis Skillicorn's B.B.C. series called 'The New Foresters'. Friday, 3rd April, 1981, is a day she will never forget. That evening the programme was shown and even before the credits finished rolling, her telephone began to ring. It didn't stop until 1.20 the next morning.

Letters poured in from would-be buyers of her paintings, some simply addressed to 'The Lady who Paints the New Forest'. Two days later, when Monica arrived to hang paintings for a local exhibition, she was astonished to find a queue of people waiting outside. It was Monica they were waiting to see. Fifteen minutes television time had produced a reaction which stayed at madness pitch for weeks.

Such a meteoric rise to stardom is a phenomenon some people cannot cope with, but not Monica Coleman. A practical woman, just turned forty, she was determined not to waste the opportunity which had so suddenly burst upon her. Monica now stages five or six exhibitions a year and the canvasses sell so fast she seldom shows a picture more than once. She believes that people like her work because they understand it.

"Art critics will tell you that realism is unfashionable but it is the realism of my paintings

that ordinary people, the man in the street, appreciate and like. They want to see things depicted as they are and that is exactly what I try and do. I paint out of a love for nature and I try to put its colours on canvas just as it really is. Somehow I am able to transmit the love I have for the Forest to the person looking at my painting."

The story of her overnight rise to fame began early in 1980 when she had a number of New Forest paintings hanging in a Forest pub just outside Ringwood. A television producer, John Coleman (no relation although he too comes from Ringwood), was having a drink there with his wife. Their conversation turned to the new series he was planning called 'The New Foresters', and his wife, having already admired the paintings, suggested that he include an artist in the series. Taken with the idea, the producer had to test Monica's feelings about the Forest and he decided to telephone her.

"One evening the telephone rang. The caller said he was a businessman from Southampton, that he liked my work and wanted me to paint a picture of his block of offices. I said it wasn't really my forté but I could give him the names of other artists who could do that sort of thing. He insisted he wanted me. Again I told him I only painted the New Forest.

'What's so special about this Forest?' he asked. 'Why don't they cut down all the trees and build on it?' Up until that point I had tried to be patient but now I got cross. I prattled on about the Forest and how if it had not been for the Forest I would not be an artist. Little did I know I was saying exactly the things he wanted to hear! When he said he was a television producer and wanted to feature me in his series, I didn't believe a word of it. I felt sure it was my friend, Graham Nolan, a local potter. We were always playing practical jokes on one another. It wasn't until John Coleman arrived at my front door and I saw 'B.B.C.' emblazoned on his car, that I really believed him!"

The day for filming dawned and despite Monica's initial nervousness, all went well. They found a spot beside a stream which suited the television crew and Monica set up her easel and began to paint, standing with one foot in a hole and the other on the bank. They filmed the creation of the painting from start to finish and later visited a local exhibition of Monica's work. It was a long day, from 10 a.m. to 6 p.m., but one of the most memorable Monica can remember.

The week after 'The New Foresters' was televised, Monica was due to hang paintings for an exhibition at Beales, the department store in Bournemouth. Unbeknown to her, the store's switchboard had been jammed with calls from people wanting details of her exhibition. Stepping out of the lift with her paintings in a large skip and accompanied by her business partner Thelma Gould, and friend Bob Whitlock, she found the way to the gallery area completely blocked by people.

"I thought there had been an accident and went to ask an assistant what had happened. 'They're waiting for Monica Coleman,' she said. I couldn't believe it. I thought the whole world had gone mad! The exhibition wasn't even due to open until the following day and here were people shaking my hand, patting me on the back and asking for autographs. I was even stopped in the street and asked to sign a Bournemouth brochure!"

The exhibition was so successful, Beales extended it from two to three weeks. All the paintings sold within the first few days and as Monica had to attend the exhibition, Thelma's daughter Susan gathered in paintings from other galleries to keep the exhibition going. Monica learnt very quickly the extraordinary effect of appearing on television. One day a lady spoke to her as though she had known Monica and her family all her life. Monica could not place her and when she hesitatingly asked her how they knew one another, the lady replied that Monica had spent fifteen minutes in her lounge only the other evening. She meant, of course, on television.

Monica's work is untrammelled by formal training but an artistic streak runs in her family. Her father, George Coleman, was a skilled artist who taught at the Bournemouth College of Art in the days when it was housed in a black tin hut in Drummond Road, Boscombe. It is thanks to her father that Monica believes she is able to see a scene and transfer it into a picture, but sadly he never lived to see her become an artist.

"As a child he would take me out for walks and insist I stand still for what seemed like hours to drink in a scene. Being young, I was impatient but something of what he was trying to show me sank in. He taught me how to see beyond the obvious, to see form, shape, light, shade and colour. I remember how excited he would get looking at something quite ordinary like a buttercup, the leaf from a tree or the patterns of water. His intense feelings about nature surprised me at the time but I now know just how he felt because I share those feelings; he has been dead for over thirty years and yet seems closer to me now than ever before."

George and Lilian Coleman

Monica's parents, George and Lilian Coleman, had been married some years before she was born on 25th October, 1934. Lilian was then in her late thirties and George was over forty, but they never seemed old to Monica. Her brother Barry had been born five years earlier and they were delighted to have a little girl to keep him company. Lilian looked forward to dressing-up her daughter in ribbons, lace and satin, little realising that Monica would grow up to be a tomboy, running around with a local gang of boys (Bob Whitlock, Norman Day, Reggie Ansell, Brian 'Titch' Ward and Bob's little brother, Ted) and getting into more scrapes than her brother. She could hold her own with any boy as an uncle took delight in teasing Lilian by teaching Monica to box and use bad language. Wearing dungarees and climbing trees was much more her line than donning a dress and playing with Betty, her doll. Even today, Monica favours the casual dress of trousers and blouses, saying she prefers comfort to swank.

"I would never make the front page of Vogue! In that way I am just like my father. I remember him always in a grey flannel suit but looking more artistic than smart. He had dark, silky hair which he wore long, right over the collar of an open-necked cream shirt and he used to roll back the sleeves of his jacket so you could see the blue and white striped lining. In those days people smoked more than they do now and he was no exception. Invariably, he had a Players untipped cigarette in his mouth. He was a quiet man and his dark brown eyes seemed permanently half-closed as though he was weighing up a scene before painting a picture."

The artistic career of Monica's father broke a family tradition of becoming cobblers. For generations the Colemans had followed this trade, living in Dulverton, Devon. Monica's grandfather, Tom, learnt the trade but longed to see more of the world. When a band of travelling minstrels came to Dulverton and asked him to join them, he could not resist. He travelled all over the country until he came to Colchester and there met Sophia, a flaxen-haired beauty who he saw for the first time swinging on a garden gate. They married and after a number of years finally settled in Bournemouth where Tom set up a boot-making business in Grantham Road, Boscombe.

Monica's memories of her grandparents are vivid. She adored her grandfather Tom who had picked up entertaining skills in his travelling minstrel days. Monica remembers him as a great song and dance man and to this day her favourite screen hero is Gene Kelly, a choice she is sure must have been influenced by her grandfather!

Tom and Sophia Coleman had five children — Della, Florence, George (Monica's father), William and Arthur. Although they all married, only George and Bill had sons and it is Bill's grandson, Lionel, who will carry on the Coleman name. Arthur's grand-daughter Sophie Emma New is named after his mother. The family can see great similarities between Sophie Emma and Monica, and the two have a close affinity. They both share the same star sign, Scorpio, a coincidence which Monica believes contributes to the bond between them.

Monica never knew her grandparents — the Murrays — on her mother Lilian's side of the family, for they died before she was born. Lilian, however, had three sisters and two brothers and Monica often sees her cousins (Aunt Maggie Linford's children) who live in London.

George Coleman, Monica's father, showed promise from an early age for he was always drawing pictures. His talent came to the notice of a wealthy widow to whom he delivered papers and so impressed was she by the budding artist that she offered to pay for him to go to art college. For George it must have been a dream come true. In later years, his creative abilities took him down other avenues but painting was his first love. He never exhibited or sold his paintings (mainly portraits and pictures of flowers) and almost all his work is still in the family. One of Monica's favourites is a delicate watercolour drawing of her grandfather which hangs on her sitting room wall.

Watercolour painting of his father, by George Coleman.

Whilst teaching at the Bournemouth College of Art, George took photography under his wing. Seeing the business potential in it, he set up his own studio in Boscombe Arcade and bought the franchise for beach photography, then in its infancy. With his young wife, Lilian, he soon built up a flourishing enterprise. George's speciality was studio portraits and Lilian, who was

meticulous in all she did, became an expert technician in the dark room developing pictures. They made a good team and worked hard and long hours.

George never forgot his benefactress or her daughter Monica. It seemed only natural when George and Lilian's baby girl was born that they should name her Monica too in honour of the family who had altered the course of George's life.

By the time Monica came along the Colemans lived in a beautiful bungalow called 'Riverbend' on the River Stour at Christchurch. George built the bungalow himself with the help of a friend, Stan Kermode, then a jobbing builder who had a trailer pulled by his bike and later to become a well-known councillor. The situation was a sentimental choice because in their courting days, George and Lilian had spent many hours walking by the river and having cream teas at nearby Bosley Farm House. Initially they bought two plots of land but when George began the footings, he was told he had put them in the wrong place so he had to buy more land and ended up with five plots. George's design for picturesque 'Riverbend' included a heather-thatched summerhouse with oak beams and crazy paving steps leading down the steep bank to the river. He also had a 'den' near the house over which roses and clematis climbed in profusion.

In 1936, George and Lilian expanded their business and moved the studio to 689 Christchurch Road near the old Carlton Cinema in Boscombe. During the busy summer season the family lived in a flat above the studio and George's brother, Arthur (who had been taken into the business), lived in the flat next door.

Those early childhood days are filled with happy memories for Monica. They were able to have assistance in the house and Monica has great affection for Edna Pike, who came to live with the family when she was sixteen years old as a nanny for Barry and a helper for Lilian. Edna wore the black dress, frilled white apron and little cap of a maid, but she became more like a sister to Monica and they are still in close touch today.

Barry and Monica with Edna.

Lilian was a devoted mother and wife, always anxious to have things just right for George. She was an ideal business partner for him, never losing her temper or becoming cross even when provoked; she was the velvet glove and George was the iron hand. Her time was divided between studio and home, and Monica remembers being fascinated by her fingers which were stained brown by photographic chemicals.

"I can see now how thoroughly she spoilt me. The house was her pride and joy and she loved working in it, never making me do anything to help. I was dreadfully untidy but she was always there behind me to clear up. The only times I remember her getting upset were when Barry and I quarrelled, which, like most brothers and sisters we did often. She would become really agitated until we stopped."

With the outbreak of World War II in 1939, George moved the family away from Bournemouth to Somerset. They rented a cottage at Porlock with a stream running through the garden. An old villager taught Monica how to tickle trout and she spent hours by the stream watching the fish, occasionally catching one and then throwing it back. George undertook the children's education and Monica remembers many of the things he taught her as freshly as if it were yesterday.

"I was always a little in awe of him as he seemed to have so much knowledge and so many talents. To me he was a genius as there was nothing he could not do. He made learning an enjoyable pastime and I particularly loved it when he took us out on nature treks. It was during those early years that I developed a love of animals and the world about me under his guiding hand."

They returned to 'Riverbend' in Christchurch a few months before the war ended. Then ten years old, Monica was sent to school for the first time and she did not enjoy the experience. She showed no particular academic promise and could not wait to leave at the age of fourteen. George, however, had plans for his young daughter, and recognising her artistic talent, arranged for her to train as an art teacher at Bournemouth College. Monica was headstrong and impatient, and soon become bored with learning basic design work. Hardly before the course had begun, she gave it up and went into the family business.

Monica was then about fifteen years old and the hectic life of beach photography suited her. She quickly learnt dark room techniques from her mother and became part of the beach team known as 'Movie Films'. They had the licence for prime positions from Southbourne through to Alum Chine including Bournemouth Pier, and a kiosk on the front where photographs

were displayed. It was a 24 hour service and with several thousand 'snaps' being taken, processed and sold in a day, they worked from 5 a.m. to 11 o'clock at night.

BOURNEMOUTH BEACH PHOTOGRAPHER
OFFICIAL LICENSEE TO THE CORPORATION

GEORGE COLEMAN
BOURNEMOUTH PIER

"We never seemed to stop running and had a dark room in the ladies' toilet where films could be changed without delay. I roped in friends to give a hand and we had a great working team. They were frantic days but we had a lot of good times."

Among Monica's close friends who remember those exhilarating and exhausting summers are Bob Whitlock, Hazel Saunders (now Jackson), Dawn D'Arcy and Wendy Worthington, who now all live in Ringwood. Bob was one of the gang from 'Riverbend' days who, after a spell in North Wales, returned to Hampshire and makes the frames for Monica's paintings. Hazel is Monica's walking companion and Dawn has just settled in Ringwood after many years in the Midlands. Wendy reversed the "roping-in" of old friends as Monica first met her when she came to work for 'Movie Films'.

A car was essential for beach photography to pick up films and deliver the finished prints. At seventeen, Monica learnt to drive and bought her first car, a Morris 10. She kept it for nearly ten years and even today Wendy and Bob can remember the registration number ORU 570!

At the height of the holiday season, 'Movie Films' employed

about forty people. The photographers used special cameras made by Monica's brother, Barry. The design was based on cameras George devised when he launched 'Movie Films' in the 1920s. He had realised that the essence of success in beach photography was speed and he had to overcome the problems of large-format, short-run film then in general use. His ingenious solution was to use film-maker's cameras on large tripods adapted to take one frame at a time, giving 1,000 shots on a reel of 16mm movie film — hence the name of the business.

Monica was nearly twenty-two when her father died suddenly of a heart attack on 13th September, 1956. The following spring the River Stour rose for the first time since 'Riverbend' was built and swept away the summerhouse where they had spent many happy hours. The robin which used to sit on his cap while he walked around the garden was never seen again and the clematis growing over his 'den' did not bloom after his death. Even his favourite rose began to die. The shock had a profound effect on Monica. Her mother never fully recovered and three years later she too died for no other reason than she had a broken heart.

The much loved family home 'Riverbend' became Monica's property and she continued to live there. Now a wealthy young woman, she left the world of photography to start up her own business. Through a series of misfortunes, the business crashed in 1963. She found herself faced with selling 'Riverbend' to pay her debts.

"Riverbend"

The experience was shattering and Monica found herself homeless and ill. Family and friends rallied around. At first she stayed with Richard and Valerie Speake; then with her brother, Barry, and his wife Dena. Slowly her health recovered.

In 1968, Monica began picking up the pieces of her life and moved to Ringwood. She took on a job with Geary's shop delivering groceries and meat to surrounding areas. The people she called on often wanted odd jobs done like tidying the garden, cleaning the windows and mowing lawns, so Monica helped them

out and her services were often paid for in produce. Eventually, Monica met Thelma Gould who had a flair for interior design and decorating and when Monica was asked to re-decorate a sitting room, she persuaded Thelma to do it with her. In next to no time, they were receiving dozens of orders for spring cleaning and decorating, and set up a business called 'A Woman's Touch'.

The name still exists today, but the business of 'A Woman's Touch' is entirely different. Until 1981 when television brought about the dramatic change in circumstances, Monica and Thelma were still taking on decorating work. Now both women concentrate on Monica's career as an artist. Thelma handles all the business side — organising exhibitions, ordering materials, etc. — and keeps the house running smoothly. The arrangement works well although Monica feels she is the one who has benefitted most.

"Without Thelma's encouragement I would never have started to paint at all and it is to her that I owe my success. She is always there to support me. She is my business partner, housekeeper, manager, secretary, confidante and friend. I consult her about everything and it is due to her hard work behind the scenes that I am able to get out into the Forest most days of the week. Thelma literally does everything except paint the pictures."

It was Thelma who started Monica drawing. When they first met in 1968, Thelma's two children, Susan and Russell, were small and Monica entertained them by drawing funny pictures. Thelma recognised a talent which had lain dormant for many years and she also knew that Monica would have to be coerced into drawing. Because Monica had such admiration and respect for her father's gifts as an artist, she believed she could never emulate him.

"One day we saw some black and white pictures and Thelma said to me 'You could do that. Why don't you do one for me?' So I did! I bought a scraper board and drew a picture of daisies. From that one picture stemmed my whole career as an artist."

Friends wanted scraper-board pictures of flowers, birds and portraits of their dogs. After a hard day painting and decorating Monica would come home and draw until late at night to finish commissions for people. Soon she was using her drawings to raise money for charity. Always interested in her fellow creatures, Monica involves herself in projects such as the International Fund for Animal Welfare and the Save the Children Fund. In Thelma she met a kindred spirit and at Christmas they would bring the work of 'A Woman's Touch' to a halt, hire a shop in Ringwood and sell art and crafts to raise money for local charities.

So successful was this enterprise that crafts-people asked whether Monica and Thelma would run a permanent outlet for

Thelma at her spinning wheel.

their work. When by chance a lady came in during the 1972 Christmas display and offered to rent them an old property in Gooseberry Lane, Ringwood, they took up the challenge. The work required to set it up as a gallery was more than Monica and Thelma could afford, so others were asked to participate. Eight craftsmen put in £100 each and with this capital and a lot of help and goodwill from local people, particularly Sue Chambers, Monica and Thelma launched 'The Granary'.

Open at weekends and on Wednesdays, 'The Granary' was a great success attracting nearly a thousand people on Sundays. The gallery was in two upstairs rooms reached by a wooden staircase and there was a great variety of crafts on show.

The main crafts-people were two ladies known as Anjo Pottery who made animals dressed as mice, Lisa Pride Knitwear (Sue Chambers), a spinner, two painters, a doll's house maker, a silversmith and, of course, Monica and Thelma. There were also many guest craftsmen who came and demonstrated their skills all over the building and in the lane outside. Visitors could see potters, wood carvers, jewellers, rocking horse makers, basket

makers and many items including pegdolls, collage, Dorset buttons and lace.

'The Granary' was not run for profit but as a forum for local people to show their crafts. The problems of running such a venture, however, were enormous and when extensive building work became necessary to comply with fire regulations, Monica and Thelma reluctantly closed it down.

Through the Christmas charity craft shows and the annual summer exhibition of paintings in Bournemouth Pleasure Gardens, Monica's black and white drawings were seen by many people. One who was impressed with her work was the manager of the tea rooms at Compton Acres, the ornamental gardens at Poole in Dorset, and he asked her to hang some pictures there. Monica was initially reluctant as she felt black and white drawings were not right for such a venue. His reply was, 'Well, you're a painter, aren't you? Why not paint some scenes of the gardens and I'll show those?'

Until then Monica had never tackled a 'real' painting. The only one she remembers doing was under the tuition of her father at the age of thirteen. A still-life of flowers, she signed it 'Monc', the name by which she is known to her friends, and gave it to Mrs. Kitty D'Arcy, who is still the proud owner of the picture. Before the war the D'Arcys had a gown shop called 'Dawn D'Arcy' in Boscombe next door to the Coleman Photographic Studios. Their daughter, Dawn, and Monica met when they were twelve months old and have been friends ever since.

Faced with the prospect of painting in colour, Monica was not deterred. One of her treasured mementoes was a box of her father's old paints, so she got it out, added a few new paints and bought some palette knives and brushes. She had never used a knife before but had watched Harley Crossley, a local artist, demonstrating one and liked the effect he had created. With characteristic enthusiasm she set off to paint the colourful gardens of Compton Acres.

"My first attempts were very amateur. I did them on hardboard using household undercoat. But they sold well for about £5 a painting. Fortunately, on my birthday, someone gave me a canvas and I began to realise what painting was all about."

It was not long before Monica cast about for other scenes to paint and the New Forest was the obvious choice. She had begun visiting it as a child with her parents and had continued to go there ever since to walk the dogs or simply to have a break from working.

Setting foot in the Forest as an artist, however, was quite different from her earlier excursions. It changed her life in more ways than one and marked a point where a healing process began.

For many years following the failure of her business, Monica suffered destructive feelings of guilt over losing everything her parents had worked so hard to achieve. As her skill and success as an artist grew, so those feelings subsided and she is now at peace with herself and feels she has vindicated the faith her father had in her ability. Indeed, she sometimes feels he is with her when she paints in the Forest and has come across strange coincidences linking the past with the present. One such event occurred when Mr. and Mrs. Stanley Baker from Bournemouth arrived at her gallery to choose a picture which their son was buying them as a golden wedding anniversary present. In conversation, Monica discovered, to their delight, that their wedding photographs had been taken by her father.

Monica's first exhibition of New Forest paintings was held in 1975 at the Goya Studios in Christchurch. In 1976, she was invited to exhibit for three weeks at Rhinefield House, a New Forest mansion then owned by Oliver Cutts and open to the public. The exhibition proved so popular it stayed for over four years.

When Monica reached the age of 43, her thoughts turned to the future. Home decorating was a physically demanding occupation and Monica saw that neither she nor Thelma could do it forever. She had long had her eye on an old property in Parsonage Barn Lane called 'Allward'. When it came up for sale in 1978, it was time to act. Although near derelict, it had plenty of rooms, making it ideal for a bed and breakfast business. She put the idea to Thelma and within a few months they pooled resources and became the owners of 'Allward'.

They took on a mammoth task as little had been done to the property for years. It is, in fact, two dwellings — one Georgian and the other an 800 year old cottage, which were joined together at some time in the past. They discovered that the cottage had been known as Pound Cottage as the person who lived there looked after the pound for stray New Forest ponies. If ponies went into private property they could be taken to the pound and the owners would have to pay a small fine to release them.

Renovating 'Allward' gave Monica and Thelma plenty of scope to put their ideas into practice. They took out and bricked-up four fireplaces, rebuilt two others, pulled down two rotten ceilings and replaced them, exposed old beams, relaid floors, mixed concrete and replaced windows so heavy to lift they had to build brick steps up to the hole! It was back-breaking work which they did on their own at weekends and in the evenings after a day's work. But it was great fun and often when something went wrong they would collapse into fits of laughter, covered in plaster dust and paint, wondering why they had been so crazy as to take the place on!

Gradually the rambling thirteen-room house took shape and the bed and breakfast business became a possibility. It was never to come about because of the events of 1981 but 'Allward' has proved ideal as a base for Monica's painting and today is a comfortable home with lots of character. Two rooms have been turned into a gallery where Monica holds exhibitions and where people can see her work by appointment. In the lounge, pride of place on the wall goes to the picture of Dockens Water which Monica painted for 'The New Foresters'.

Upstairs is her studio, a large room full of canvasses, paintings, frames, work benches and an easel near the window. Monica spends little time here, except in the winter, as almost all her canvasses are painted on location. The only details she will put in when she returns home are animals. Deer are too elusive to paint from life and she uses a large collection of colour photographs taken on her walks. During the cold and wet months of winter when it is impossible to go outside, she paints canvasses from her photographs.

The house is often full of people as Monica is gregarious by nature and has a close circle of long-standing friends. Most, like Bob Whitlock and Hazel Jackson, she has known for thirty years or more and Thelma she met nearly twenty years ago. Their friendship and loyalty is deeply valued. Without the support she had from Thelma and Bob, Monica says she would never have survived the rush of publicity which followed her television appearance. It is due in great part to her friends, and particularly to Thelma, that Monica believes she owes the richly rewarding and fulfilling life she enjoys today.

Deer watching with Hazel.

A love of animals is part of Monica's life and she maintains that if a person cannot love an animal, then he cannot love anything at all. This has led her to become a vegetarian and to support causes for the protection of certain animals. It creates problems when she is painting because insects sometimes fly into the paint and get trapped. She cannot bear to see them die and spends precious time rescuing them, wiping them off and letting them go.

Monica has had her own dog since early childhood and every one is special to her. She has often taken in dogs for friends who are no longer able to care for them and remembers, with great affection, Molly a black labrador, who came when her owner died.

"One of my earlier dogs was a poodle called Susie. When I sat in the car, she would lie around my shoulders like a warm scarf! Cindy, another black labrador, was the dog who appeared in 'The New Foresters' with me. She was only eight weeks old when we had her and she was a perfect dog from the start. The only thing she ever chewed as a puppy was her bed which she happily shared with Honey the cat. She was a patient dog and never made any fuss. She was also very affectionate and loved Thelma and Russell as much, if not more, than me. She died in 1984 at the age of 14 and left a big hole in my life which can never be completely filled."

Monica with Cindy.

Monica's new dog, Sika — named after a type of New Forest deer — is also a black labrador but has quite a different character. Full of energy, she is a vociferous guard dog and has proved difficult to train. Unlike Cindy who plodded along and never disappeared from view, Sika is full of mischief and keeps Monica on her toes. She needs lots of exercise and Monica takes her when walking in the Forest.

With a full schedule of painting and walking, Monica has little time to spare and has never been interested in going on holiday. She calls herself a "home-bird" and enjoys being involved in local events. In 1986 she was invited to become a trustee of The Meeting House in Ringwood, a centre for local people interested in the arts, which houses a museum of old Ringwood and stages exhibitions.

Monica participates every year in the New Forest Show where she demonstrates her painting techniques. She also exhibits throughout the area but seldom goes further than a day's drive away from the Forest.

"I like to attend my exhibitions because it means more to people if they actually meet the artist and talk about the place depicted in the painting they want to buy. The disadvantage is that I can't get out in the Forest and if a season is short-lived, like autumn when a storm can whip the leaves off overnight, I'm not able to paint many pictures before it is over."

Three years ago Monica began exploring the Forest in earnest. Previously she went everywhere by car, seldom venturing deep into the woods because painting gear is heavy to carry. Once she left the painting tools behind and started walking, a whole new dimension of the Forest opened up to her. This increased awareness is visible in recent canvasses which have even greater strength and beauty than before.

Monica rarely goes into the Forest alone and her companions on painting expeditions are usually Thelma or Hazel Jackson. On long walks she is always accompanied by Hazel. Once Monica became a full-time artist and wanted to spend more time in the Forest, Hazel suggested they take up walking. It would be a good way of keeping fit, exercising the dogs, exploring areas they had never visited before and finding unusual scenes for paintings.

"Neither of us had done proper walking before and I'll never forget our first attempt. It was in May 1983 and it nearly killed me. But I persevered and now I can walk 14 miles on a fine summer's day although I still find it hard going up hills. There's no doubt it's made me a fitter person and it's given me hours of pleasure because I've discovered so much in the Forest I never knew about before. I shall be eternally grateful to Hazel for bullying me into that first walk."

Equipped with proper walking gear, Monica and Hazel are out in the Forest at least two days a week. Fascinated by deer which they encountered on early morning walks, they have studied these gentle creatures for over two years and are well versed in their habits and behaviour. Deer often appear in Monica's paintings although sometimes you have to look twice before spotting them, so well do they merge into the background, just as they do in real life.

Monica's interest in deer and their well being has led her to become an active member of the New Forest Deer Protection Council. Formed in January 1985, the Council seeks to abolish the activities of the New Forest Buckhunt which annually chases over thirty deer to exhaustion using a pack of hounds. Monica is not a saboteur nor does she follow the hunt to interfere with it in any way. Her own experiences show what a devastating effect the hunt has on the Forest.

"If you go through the Forest a few hours or even a day after the hunt, there isn't a bird making a sound. The whole Forest seems paralysed with a solid wall of fear. There are notices saying 'Dogs must be on a lead' yet thirty baying hounds are allowed to crash through the undergrowth disturbing anything in their path as they chase a terrified deer, sometimes to its death. And it is done simply to provide fun for members of the Buckhunt."

Recently, Monica began her own column, a New Forest Diary, in the Newsletter of the Deer Protection Council. The discipline of writing down her observations seemed a natural extension for her feelings about the Forest and she finds it another satisfying way of expressing them.

Living in Ringwood, Monica has only a few minutes drive to be in the Forest and her daily programme is governed by its rhythms and the passage of the seasons. Even in the leisure hours of evening, Monica's thoughts are in the Forest. Although she seldom does pen and ink work these days, she has returned to this medium to produce all the drawings, maps and decorative borders for this book.

"People have asked why I seldom paint anywhere but the Forest and my reply is that I'm not interested in painting anything but the Forest because it is the

Forest alone that inspires me. It is the most wonderful place in the world and I try and put my feelings about it into my pictures. Sometimes I feel I have failed but on other occasions I know I have struck the right note. I remember one exhibition at Greyfriars in Ringwood a few years ago when a retired couple from New Zealand kept coming back to look at my pictures. They were interested in one of Moyles Court, one of my favourite places, and we began talking. She had known and loved Moyles Court as a child and to my surprise tears came into her eyes. 'I knew it was a special place for you too,' she said. 'Because I could feel your love for it coming to me through the painting.'"

Monica's pictures hang in homes around the world from Iceland to Australia. People who do not know the area but who saw her in 'The New Foresters' have been so entranced with her work they have come to Hampshire and sought her out. With a painting tucked under an arm, they have gone off into the Forest to find the location where it was painted. If they experience even a fraction of the pleasure that Monica gains from the Forest she is well pleased for she feels it repays something of what the Forest has given her.

"The New Forest acts on me like a magical balm which puts all the mundane problems of life into perspective and sweeps away every trouble. Each time I paint there I try to catch some of its mystery and beauty on canvas, but how can you capture something as unique, perfect and elusive as nature? I shall go on trying until the day I die."

The New Forest

If William the Conqueror were to see one of Monica Coleman's paintings he would instantly identify it as the New Forest. In contradiction to its name, the New Forest is Britain's oldest forest and was created by King William as a royal hunting ground in about 1079. In over a thousand years little has changed in parts of the Forest and this sense of timelessness adds to the magnetism which first attracted Monica to the Forest.

Covering some 93,000 acres of woodland, heath and plantation, the New Forest encompasses most of southern Hampshire. It stretches from Monica's doorstep just outside Ringwood, to the boundary with Wiltshire in the north, to Beaulieu in the west and to the sea coast in the south. Within its 145 square mile border is widely differing scenery ranging from oak, beech and holly woods to heather-covered heath, and from wet bogland to dark conifer plantations.

The New Forest is part of Britain's national heritage and is managed by the Forestry Commission. Remarkably, it has survived the march of time and has a vast reservoir of wildlife which includes some of Britain's rarest plants and creatures. In the following pages some of these wonders of nature have been drawn by Monica including the seldom-seen sand lizard, the purple emperor butterfly and the Dartford warbler.

Today the Forest is criss-crossed by busy trunk roads which serve the local communities and a thriving tourist industry. There are camp sites, barbecue areas, specially sign-posted walks and picnic areas, yet it is still possible to get off the beaten track and feel you are the only person for miles around.

The oldest parts of the Forest are the Ancient and Ornamental Woodlands, some 8,000 acres of oak, beech and holly. Protected by law, they contain some of the finest specimens of oak and beech to be seen in Britain and have remained virtually the same for centuries. They feature in Monica's paintings and their beauty is unsurpassed no matter what time of year. The delicate colours of winter can be seen in the paintings of Brinken and Pinnick Woods, and Rhinefield is depicted with the glorious colours of autumn.

Quite different are the wide expanses of heath, gorse and bog known as Open Forest where self-seeded Scots pines raggedly pierce the horizon. There are also 22,000 acres of enclosed plantations where trees are grown as timber. The painting of North Oakley Inclosure is within one of these plantations, which are fenced to prevent animals from damaging young trees.

In this ancient yet living landscape, laws and rights first introduced in medieval times are still in force today. Roaming the open forest are ponies, cattle, pigs and donkeys belonging to people known as Commoners. They live in houses which have special privileges called Rights of Common. The most valued of these is the right to graze animals freely, a practice believed to date from Norman times when great hardship was brought upon farmers who were prohibited by law from fencing their land. Other rights allow the collection of firewood, the cutting of peat and turning out pigs during the pannage season to eat acorns and beech nuts (known as mast).

To ensure that the harsh Forest laws were kept, King William set up special courts. A remnant of those long-past days still survives in the Verderers' Court which regularly sits in Lyndhurst, capital of the New Forest. One of its chief duties is to supervise the Commoners' animals and collect payment for every animal grazing in the Forest.

The sturdy New Forest pony, a breed older than the Forest itself, is very much part of the Forest landscape and can be seen in the painting of Anses Wood. By grazing in the same area for hundreds of years, the ponies have helped give the Forest its distinctive expanses of smooth green grass and open glades. These semi-wild animals are all owned by Commoners and live not only on grass but also on gorse, brambles, bark and holly which is found in abundance in the Forest. Sadly, some of the ponies do not survive harsh winters because the hardiness of the New Forest pony has been weakened over the years by the introduction of other breeds.

The Forestry Commission took over management of the New Forest in 1924. To them falls the difficult task of looking after all the different interests in the Forest — their own as growers of timber, the Verderers, the Commoners, private landowners, thousands of holiday-makers and many others — which they do in consultation with the Nature Conservancy Council. From many hours spent in the Forest, Monica has seen how the Commission does its work and pays tribute to the way in which it carries out its obligations and has preserved the traditional character of the Forest.

Monica also has praise for the way in which the wildlife is protected. The Forest is famous for its badger setts hidden deep in the woods, its foxes which are often seen during the day and, most particularly, its deer — the true aristocrats of the Forest. Lingering in the shadows of trees, basking in sunshine, grazing on heath, bounding across a meadow, deer are found throughout the Forest. Often elusive, always fascinating, a glimpse of them is the most sought-after prize for visitors. Without them the New Forest would never have come into existence, and without them the New Forest would never have survived.

The Deer of the New Forest

The New Forest began its life as a royal hunting ground when William the Conqueror wanted to pursue his favourite sport and the animal he hunted was deer. So much did he enjoy this pastime that he imposed swingeing laws on the Forest which took little account of the people who lived there and were designed to protect the deer. Even the trees were of little importance except as natural cover for his animals.

Throughout medieval times, punishment for breaking Forest laws was harsh. There was even a special law to protect deer from being worried by dogs. Every dog belonging to a person living in the Forest had to pass through the Stirrup of Rufus and if it was too large to do so, had to undergo a maiming practice called expeditation — amputating its front claws. The stirrup can still be seen in the Verderers' Hall at Lyndhurst.

Charles II was the last monarch to show interest in the Forest as a hunting ground. During his reign the Forest's herd of red deer was replenished by sixty stags, the gift of the King of France. By the end of the century, however, its use for the provision of oak timber for building ships at Portsmouth and Bucklers Hard, Beaulieu, became the priority of the day.

In 1707 it became obvious that the woodlands were badly depleted but it was not until 1808 that an extensive programme of planting oaks began. Proposals were made to enclose vast areas for growing timber in the Forest and in 1851 a Deer Removal Act was passed. The outcry by Commoners resulted in the New Forest Act of 1877 being passed which laid the foundation for the administration of the Forest as it is today and limits the acreage of land used for timber growing.

Fortunately, it proved impossible to slaughter all the deer. Several thousand were killed but a few managed to survive in the dense thickets of the Forest. Eventually, they were left alone and gradually the herds began to re-establish themselves although the Act remained in force until 1971.

Since the early 16th century, the men responsible for looking after deer were the Keepers — and so it is today. Each keeper has his own area of the Forest, usually lives within that area and knows it intimately. Through her observations of deer and long walks, Monica is known to a number of keepers whom she has always found extremely helpful and brimming over with knowledge about the Forest.

The keeper is responsible for everything that goes on in his beat from visitors to wild animals but much of his work revolves around managing the deer. Every April, he spends hours making a census of deer because their number is strictly controlled. If you come across strange tower-like structures in the Forest, these are not observation platforms for the public but high-seats used for the count and the annual deer cull.

Distressing though the shooting of deer is, Monica acknowledges that culling is essential to preserve the health of the herds and to prevent the number rising to such an extent that it would exceed the winter feed. Although she has not seen a keeper shooting, Monica knows when the cull takes place and has heard the sharp retort of a high velocity rifle echoing around the Forest. One crack — then silence. The keepers are expert shots, know exactly which animals they have to shoot and do so with a single bullet.

At night keepers watch their beat for poachers. Venison is highly prized game meat and the only time it is legally available is during the cull. Poachers usually come by night with lurchers and use lights to blind the deer. The dog is set off to bring the animal to ground but often this goes wrong and animals are not killed outright and escape badly mauled. Thanks to the vigilance of the keepers, the police and the Deer Protection Council, poaching in the Forest is kept to a minimum. If you should see anything suspicious do not hesitate to report it to the police.

Sometimes a confrontation with poachers can be an ugly and frightening experience. One keeper remembers a time when he tracked down two men to a place where they had set up a tent for the night. They were armed with shot-guns and were not at all pleased at being discovered. The situation was only diffused by the timely arrival of the police. At the other end of the intruder scale, he had earlier been called upon to remove a snake from the kitchen of a terrified Forest dweller.

Today, there are probably some 2,000 deer in the Forest of five different types — red, fallow, sika, roe and muntjac. The most commonly seen are fallow and they can be easily watched at Bolderwood Sanctuary. You can either observe them from the platforms or simply look over the fence. Usually the females, who do not have antlers, keep in a separate group from the males who will probably be grazing close by.

A number of terms peculiar to deer are used to describe them. Some which may be helpful are:

Stag	—	red or sika male
Buck	—	fallow or roe male
Hind	—	red or sika female
Doe	—	fallow or roe female
Calf	—	red or sika young
Fawn	—	fallow young
Kid	—	roe young

Rut	—	the mating season
Pricket	—	male deer with first head of antlers
Pelage	—	coat of a deer
Tines	—	points on an antler
Velvet	—	skin covering a growing antler
Fraying	—	act of rubbing off velvet on vegetation such as young trees

Each type of deer has quite distinctive features but when seen in the wild can be hard to identify. It takes many years of familiarity with all five types to instantly recognise them, particularly when in shadow or under trees where sunlight ripples through moving leaves enhancing their camouflage markings. The following are descriptions from Monica's own observations:

Red Deer

Red deer are Britain's largest wild animal and are often as big as horses. There are probably about 40 roaming the Forest, moving in small herds of ten animals or so. They are the original natives of the Forest but nearly became extinct and even now seem to be struggling to survive. In winter they can be seen out on the open expanses of heathland enjoying sunshine in full view of passing traffic.

Their coats in summer are a rich dark red and they have a creamy rump area with a fat tail. In winter, their colour becomes more grey. Females often have fawn-coloured coats with dark, almost black hairs running from the top of the tail area right down the sides of their legs, on the elbows of their front legs and along their bellies, with a tail area so pale it looks almost bald.

Stags have the classic branching antlers and in winter develop a prominent mane. Antlers are cast about March and the rut is in September and October. Calves are born in June and have a sprinkling of white spots which fade after six weeks.

Fallow Deer

Fallow are the most numerous deer in the Forest and probably number around 1,300. They are thought to have been introduced by the Normans. In summer they have a pretty chestnut coat dappled with prominent white spots. In winter these disappear when the coat darkens to an almost mulberry colour. The under-parts are always very light and they have a long tail, about nine inches, which they flick to keep off flies. Their white rumps are edged with a black line which goes right down the tail almost in the shape of a capital 'T', and along the back.

Fallow have antlers quite different from red deer and mature bucks have huge, palmated antlers. They rise up in a curve, the flattened part twisting inwards, like the graceful arms of a ballet dancer. Fallow cast their antlers in April and a new head grows ready for the rut in October.

Roe Deer

Roe were one of the original natives of the Forest but became extinct during the middle ages, only re-establishing themselves in the 19th century after some were released into the wild from Milton Abbas in Dorset. They now number a few hundred and are easily distinguished from other deer when they turn their backs and run away because they are the only deer in the Forest not to have a tail.

The summer coat is bright fox-red with a buff coloured rump-patch which is not, like fallow and sika, edged in black. Roe have large, black-rimmed ears and the face is blunter than other deer with a pale chin-patch. In winter, the coat thickens to grey-brown and the rump area becomes pure white.

Bucks have branching antlers which they shed in November or December. A new set is grown by the following May.

The roe rut normally falls between mid-June and mid-August and they have a remarkable feature known as delayed implantation. An ova fertilised in summer can lay dormant until late December when it will begin to grow ready for birth the following May. Many roe give birth to twins.

Sika Deer

Sika deer are native to Japan and those in the Forest are descendants of four animals released from the Beaulieu Manor Estate in the early 1900s. There are probably around 80 sika in the Forest, all living in the Brockenhurst area.

Smaller than fallow, sika have a bright chestnut summer coat with yellowish-white spots. These spots are not so distinctive as fallow and they also have a row of white spots each side of a dark stripe running down the back and tail. In winter their coats are sooty grey with a soft mink colour down their necks.

Sika look as though they are frowning because they have a 'U'-shaped white band above the eyes. They have a white rump area rimmed with black and a short tail.

Stags have branching antlers, similar to red deer, which they cast about April.

Muntjac Deer

Muntjac are the most timid, secretive and seldom seen type of deer in the Forest. No-one knows how many there are and they probably only arrived in the last ten to fifteen years. Originally liberated from Woburn Park about 1900, they are indigenous to south-east Asia but seem to like our climate and have flourished in woodlands throughout the centre of England.

The antlers of a muntjac are quite different from other deer. They look like spiky horns which grow out of long, hairy pedicles (raised portions of the skull above the eye) and are laid back, almost level with the neck. A new set of antlers is grown every year but not at any particular season. Muntjac have protruding upper canine teeth which they probably use for stripping bark from trees or fighting with other bucks during the rut.

The smallest of the New Forest deer, their coats are a deep rust colour with a lighter patch at the throat. The winter coat is greyer and the underparts are lighter with white on the belly and on the inside of the thighs. The tail is about six inches long and is white underneath.

Both males and females have a staccato dog-like bark when alarmed and they are particularly noisy when mating. They can mate during all months of the year and females can give birth every seven months.

*　　　*　　　*

Antlers are a male deer's glory and even though cast once a year, you will be lucky to find a set. Rich in calcium and phosphorous, antlers are often chewed by deer as soon as they shed them. They are composed of bone and when growing are covered in a soft furry skin called velvet. After four to five months when the antlers are fully grown, the velvet is removed by fraying trees to burnish and polish them. The deer is then said to be "in hard antler" in preparation for the rutting season. In the following April, the antler either falls or is knocked off and a new set begins to grow almost immediately. With each passing year, the shape becomes larger and more complex. It is said you can tell the age of a male from the number of tines but this is not reliable as many factors such as quality and quantity of food can effect the growth of antlers.

Deer are gentle, timid creatures and the only way to see them outside the sanctuary is to keep very quiet. They will often stand and stare, suspicious of a motionless object, and if you move will either bound away or continue grazing. When they run they hold their tails erect with the white underside fanned out. One of the best ways to watch them is at daybreak from an observation tower which can be hired from the Forestry Commission. Above all, you should never take a dog when you want to watch deer because they are terrified of dogs and will flee in panic, sometimes injuring themselves so badly they die in great pain.

The irony of the fact that the New Forest was created for hunting deer, a sport to which Monica is vehemently opposed, is not lost on her. She cannot, and never will, understand how people can chase, torment and kill an animal for pleasure. She is not concerned with New Forest politics but on the issue of deer hunting is prepared to "come off the fence" and campaign for its abolition. On this one subject she is at odds with the Forestry Commission who grant the licence to the New Forest Buckhunt. Despite the fact that 66 per cent of New Forest residents disapprove of deer hunting, it is still carried out twice a week from September to April, except for the month of October when fallow deer are rutting.

PART II

THE PAINTINGS

The fourteen paintings and all the drawings have been made by Monica specifically for this book. The accompanying text for each painting records experiences she has had in the Forest or which have shaped her feelings for it and the wildlife that shelters there.

She has drawn maps (not to scale) showing the location of each painting, some involving rigorous walks and others close to a car park. Along with the maps are notes on the walk and things to look for on the way or in the vicinity.

In some cases the scene may not be exactly the same as in the painting. For instance, in the one of Highland Water the ivy-covered trunk leaning across the water fell much lower with the freak snowfall in March 1987. By the end of the year it will probably be in the water. Such are the changes wrought by nature. The same painting appears on the dust-jacket but has been transposed so the deer appear on the front rather than the back.

For those interested in Monica's technique, she gives a guide to how she paints a canvas. She has also included notes of the equipment she uses or takes with her when walking, and useful tips for enjoying the Forest to the full.

Fallow bucks in autumn open Monica's personal view of the New Forest. This, for her, is the most spell-binding time of all. A time when the Forest's mantle is at its most spectacular and when the fallow buck is at its most majestic. This is when the deer come out of the shadows and become prominent in the landscape. The deer is the king of the Forest and the Forest belongs to no-one else but the deer.

Step with Monica into the magical world of the New Forest and through her eyes see it as you have never seen it before.

Monica at work.

Vinney Ridge
RHINEFIELD

25

FALLOW BUCK
IN VELVET

Vinney Ridge, Rhinefield

And I stood there breathing the beauty into my soul. The air was sweet with the smell of pine trees. Distant snorting of a rutting fallow buck penetrated the stillness. My mind exploded with excitement as I approached the sound. Then it stopped. All was quiet. I waited. Then again he bellowed out his song of existence. Nearer now. Confusing me as it echoed and rang around the old woods, almost as if all his ancestors were joining in the chorus.

Ahead I could see several does, some laying in the sun, others grazing, occasionally lifting their graceful heads to look in the direction of the snorting. I watched for some time unable to see the buck. He seemed to be working his way all around the does but staying in cover. I could hear him coming towards me. Closer he came. I was filled with fear that my very presence would spoil this wonderful scene. Still closer he came. Suddenly he was there almost behind me. He stood still listening and sniffing the air. I froze. Did he know I was there? He threw back his beautiful head, the huge antlers touching his shoulders and called to the does. He strutted past me, far too important to bother with a mere human. He stepped into the sun, the bright light dancing on his coat. His head and neck still the golden chestnut of summer mingled with coming winter greys shining silver. A familiar sight yet I was seeing it for the first time.

The does moved in to prance around him. In a fairy ring they went around and around. Like children playing a game. The great buck bellowed. They answered him with soft calls. All the time new females joined the circle. On the edge, babies with stubby antlers teetered backwards and forwards. Anxious for their mothers. What was this strange performance they had never witnessed before? The courtship ritual.

Even as autumn leaves fell, new growth was revealed, waiting, sleeping. This is the miracle of new life. So the end is the beginning.

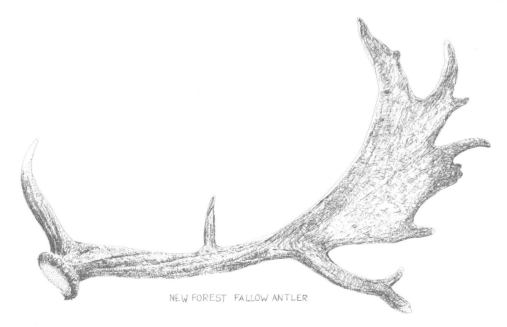

NEW FOREST FALLOW ANTLER

27

PAINTING No.1

Place: **VINNEY RIDGE, RHINEFIELD**
Time of Year: **Late October**
Length of Walk: **1½ miles**

Fallow deer are often seen in this area. One of the prettiest sights is when a group are startled and they bound away, tails upright, bouncing on all fours at high speed as though the ground beneath their feet is too hot to touch. They are not built to run for great distances and after a while will stop, look back, then run off again.

The buck in this painting is in hard antler and has long lost the velvet which protected his antlers whilst they were growing. A few months before he looked as though he had been through a haunted castle with long cobwebs festooning his antlers. Now they are burnished earth-brown ready to defend his rutting stand.

Mature bucks are wonderful to see during the rutting reason.

Their coats are at their most luxuriant, thickening to a dark colour ready for the winter months. They become aggressive and noisy. Their neck thickens, their Adam's apple swells, they urinate and anoint trees with scent glands to mark out territories. They groan with a curious grunting sound. If you have a strong sense of smell and a mature buck is in the vicinity, you will pick up the warm musty odour they develop.

The location of the painting is only a few hundred yards from Brock Hill car park and it is dry underfoot all year round. The walk back is longer and there is a gentle slope coming back to the car park.

Several Forestry Commission trails begin from this car park, and the nearby Blackwater Arboretum is interesting for those wanting to identify different trees. There are seats where you can rest.

The car park is an excellent place to see wild birds that have become tame. Monica has had bluetits, great tits and chaffinches virtually feeding from her hand. She is sure they are fed regularly in winter as she has seen a couple there with a bird-table attached to the window of their car and the birds come flying down as soon as you pull up. In nesting time, you won't see so many birds close to because they are only fed in winter. It is dangerous to feed them at other times because they become reliant on food brought to them and baby blue tits have been found choked to death by peanuts.

A little further along Rhinefield Drive towards Brockenhurst is an area called Whitefield Moor where linnets' nests can be found in gorse bushes. Linnets line their nest with feathers and Monica has watched a female pluck feathers from its breast when building a nest.

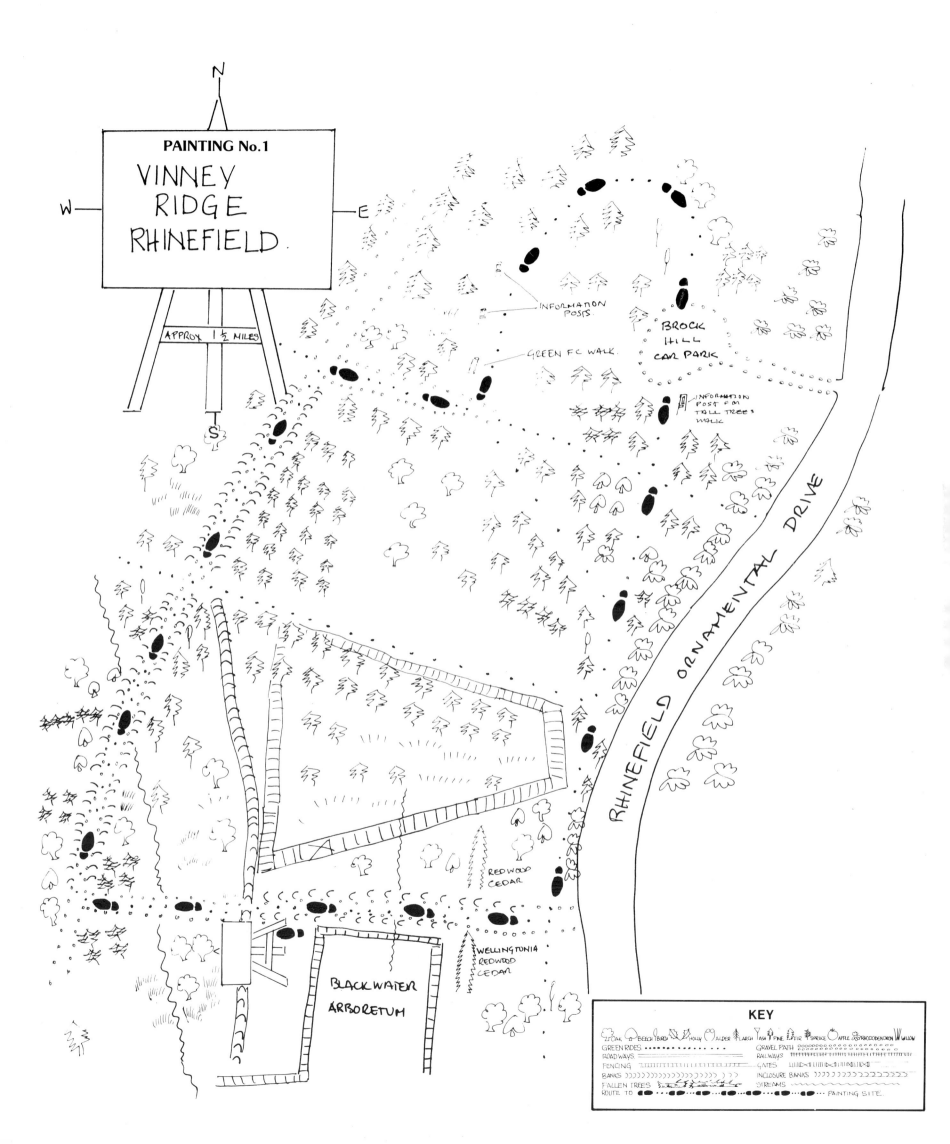

PAINTING No.1

VINNEY RIDGE RHINEFIELD.

N

W   E

S

APPROX 1½ MILES

INFORMATION POSTS

GREEN FC WALK.

BROCK HILL CAR PARK

INFORMATION POST FOR TALL TREES WALK

RHINEFIELD ORNAMENTAL DRIVE

REDWOOD CEDAR

WELLINGTONIA REDWOOD CEDAR

BLACKWATER ARBORETUM

KEY

OAK BEECH BIRCH HOLLY ALDER LARCH ASH PINE FIR SPRUCE APPLE RHODODENDRON WILLOW

GREEN RIDES ● ● ● ● ● ● ● ● ● ●   GRAVEL PATH ○○○○○○○○○○○○○○○○○○○○

ROADWAYS ═══════════════════   RAILWAYS ▦▦▦▦▦▦▦▦▦▦▦▦▦▦

FENCING ‖‖‖‖‖‖‖‖‖‖‖‖‖‖‖‖‖   GATES ‖‖‖╳‖‖‖‖╳‖‖‖‖╳‖‖‖‖

BANKS ⟩⟩⟩⟩⟩⟩⟩⟩⟩⟩⟩⟩⟩⟩⟩   INCLOSURE BANKS ⟩⟩⟩⟩⟩⟩⟩⟩⟩⟩⟩⟩⟩⟩⟩⟩⟩

FALLEN TREES ⪤⪤⪤⪤⪤⪤   STREAMS ∼∼∼∼∼∼∼∼∼

ROUTE TO ● ● ● ● ● ● ● ● ● ● ● ● ● ● ● ● ● PAINTING SITE.

Ivy Wood, Brockenhurst

Whilst being interviewed on local radio one day I said that I rarely go painting alone and confessed to having a 'donkey' to help me carry my gear. My walking companion, Hazel Jackson, lays claims to being that donkey! We walk the Forest together at least twice a week. We start the morning by having coffee while our dogs, Sika and Sally, let off steam, romping in the car park.

One early May morning we were entertained by a wren building a nest for his lady near this spot. First we saw him on the ground gathering moss and dead leaves. Then, hopping more than flying, he took his load up into ivy growing on an oak tree. A few seconds of weaving, then a song. Back to the ground, more moss, back up to the nest site. With great speed he wove. Another song and down again. Grass this time, long pieces that he used to thread and tie the moss and leaves together. A third song and so the pattern went on, weaving and singing.

We wondered if his mate would like this house. Sometimes, so I have been told, he will build two or three before madame is satisfied. A lot of energy must get wasted building unused nests but we all do funny things for love!"

WREN

Ivy Wood
BROCKENHURST

Painting No.2

OTTER.

PAINTING No.2

Place: **IVY WOOD, BROCKENHURST**

Time of Year: **Early in May**

There is no walk to the location of the painting as it can easily be seen from the car park which runs down to Lymington River (not shown in the painting). In this area sika deer can be seen.

The copse of oak, beech, ash and holly in this picture is a private one where bluebells carpet the floor untrampled by human feet. Lymington River is one of the few places in the Forest where primroses grow along the banks and where otters lived until a few years ago. Unfortunately, they are seldom seen now because they were over-hunted and their habitat has been over-taken by mink which escaped from farms. Yet another interference with the natural world by man. Elsewhere in the Forest, primroses are found on stream banks where people cannot reach.

In days gone by, Monica can remember seeing the small wild daffodil growing throughout the Forest but now only a few plants are left. Bluebells too are only found in a few areas but the heady atmosphere of a bluebell wood brings back memories for her. At 'Riverbend', the Coleman family home, bluebells grew in the dell right down to the water's edge and the whole family would gather armfuls to put in pots so the house was full of their delicious scent.

In deciduous woods like Ivy Wood, a common plant is the wood spurge which has a yellow-green leaf-like flower in the spring. There is a wealth of wild flowers in the Forest — about 700 species — but some are difficult to find as their flowering span is so short-lived.

There are hundreds of different birds to be heard and seen. One of the commonest is the chaffinch and the rarest the Dartford Warbler which is protected by law. A tiny, dark-plumaged bird with a long tail, he normally frequents the depths of gorse and makes a soft chirring sound. You can hear the birds without seeing them and after a while come to recognise their distinctive calls such as the Stonechat which sounds like two stones being knocked together. Birds of prey like the kestrel often hover motionless overhead and Monica has come across a baby Common Buzzard sitting atop a tree and watched as its mother fed it.

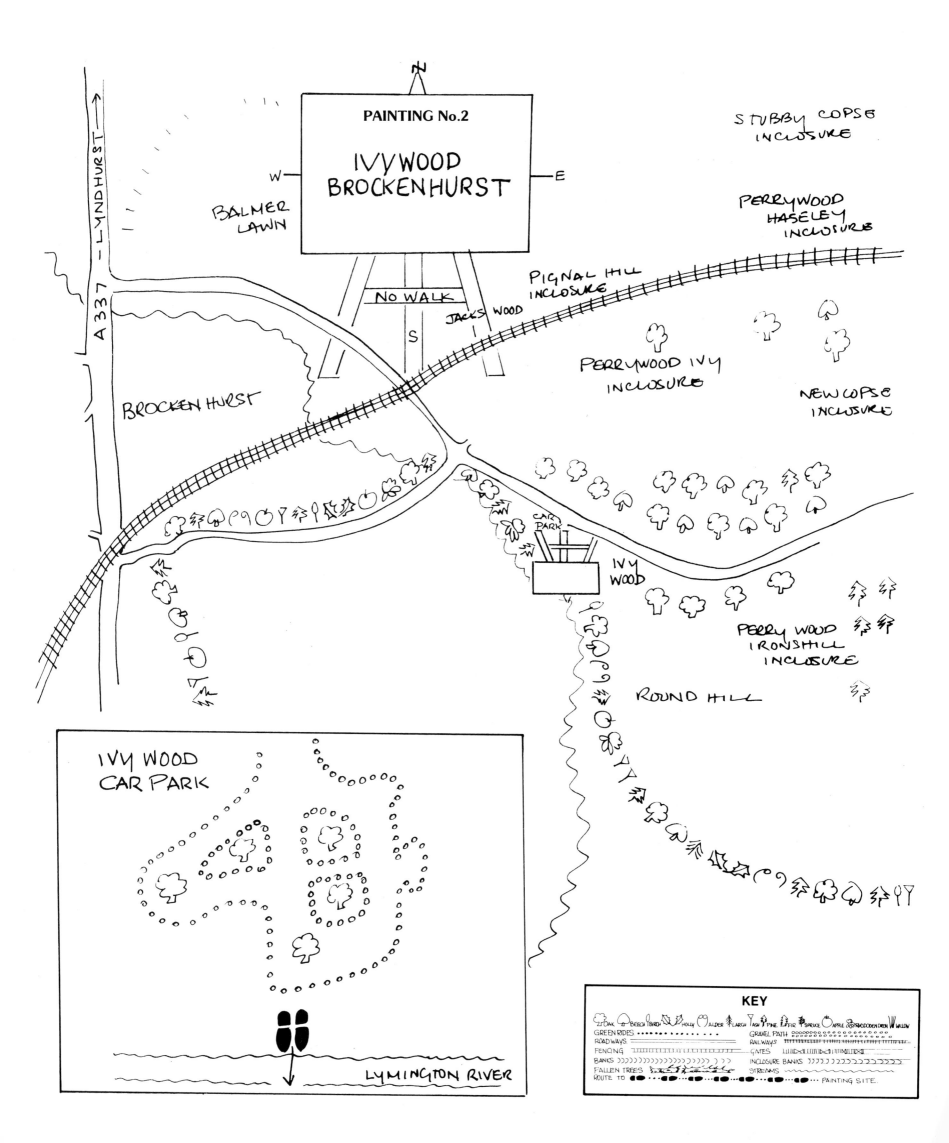

N

IVYWOOD
BROCKENHURST

W   E

S

← LYNDHURST

A337

BALMER LAWN

NO WALK

BROCKENHURST

JACKS WOOD

PIGNAL HILL INCLOSURE

STUBBY COPSE INCLOSURE

PERRYWOOD HASELEY INCLOSURE

PERRYWOOD IVY INCLOSURE

NEW COPSE INCLOSURE

CAR PARK

IVY WOOD

PERRY WOOD IRONSHILL INCLOSURE

ROUND HILL

IVY WOOD CAR PARK

LYMINGTON RIVER

KEY

OAK   BEECH   BIRCH   HOLLY   ALDER   LARCH   ASH   PINE   FIR   SPRUCE   APPLE   RHODODENDRON   WILLOW

GREEN RIDES ●●●●●●●●●   GRAVEL PATH ○○○○○○○○○

ROADWAYS ═══════   RAILWAYS ┼┼┼┼┼┼┼┼┼

FENCING ⊤⊤⊤⊤⊤⊤⊤⊤   GATES ▢▢▢▢▢▢▢

BANKS >>>>>>>>>>>>>   INCLOSURE BANKS >>>>>>>>>>>

FALLEN TREES 🌲🌲🌲   STREAMS 〰〰〰

ROUTE TO ●●●●●●●●●●●●●● PAINTING SITE

Monica and Anne Ruffell checking details of walks.

Fox cubs and vixen at the animal reserve belonging to wildlife film-maker, Eric Ashby, who lives in the New Forest.

Just for Spring

Christmas Day he was still singing. He had begun a week or more before. All through January and February too. Snow, rain, hail, freezing fog. He didn't care. Sing, sing, sing. When working at home in my studio, I usually have music on but everything went off for him — the 'Allward' song thrush.

The other birds didn't start until mid-March. That is when he stopped. Now, late April, his new family are outside yelling for food with lungs just like the old man. He made winter short for me and now I'll do my best to protect his kids.

The calling of young birds is, to me, the true sound of spring. A sound that brings pictures to one's mind of greens that the sun shines right through, of yellow daffodils and primroses; a drift of bluebells dripping with soft spring rain; dandelions and daisies; tadpoles and the occasional yellow brimstone butterfly. Beautiful tiny white flowers telling us that in autumn we'll see the bloom on the fruit of the sloe.

Spring, full of sunshine and showers. New things, young things. Foals and fawns. Curlews calling their warbling song over marshes and bogs. Bracken heads curling out of the ground like snakes. Grass appearing where only a few weeks ago the Forestry Commission burned off old gorse.

Looking this way and that as birds high in trees call, elusively and teasingly. Did I hear that song before? Is it a rare bird? So many sounds. Warblers, stonechats, linnets. Every year seems so new. The lovely sweet scented evening breezes that drift through the door at night, feeling warmer than inside the house.

Blackensford Brook
NORTH OAKLEY INCLOSURE

Painting No.3

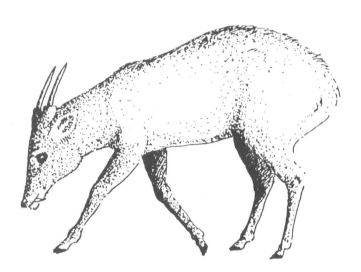

Blackensford Brook, North Oakley Inclosure

It is well into May before the bracken starts to grow. If you look close to the ground you can see lovely shapes as it forces itself up through the earth's surface to reach the sun's rays.

Bracken is not eaten by animals. Bedding is its main use for badgers, birds and mice. New Forest ponies lay up in it, as do deer. Even man used bracken as bedding not so many years ago. An inn in Brockenhurst once filled bedsize sacks with it for overnight customers. A strange, pretty, useful plant.

In summer it creates a secret forest for small animals, as well as protecting the rare wild gladioli from picking hands.

What is that movement over there? On the far side of the bank. In the bracken. Is the light playing tricks? Peeping through the fern two black eyes, a tiny nose. Too small to be a fallow or roe; too big to be a rabbit. Suddenly it springs up and scurries away. Head held low, almost hump-backed with back legs higher than the front. In a flash it is gone.

Knowing that muntjac have been officially sighted in Marsh Ash Wood, I wanted it to be a muntjac — and so it was.

BRACKEN

39

PAINTING No.3

Place:	**BLACKENSFORD BROOK,** **NORTH OAKLEY INCLOSURE**
Time of Year:	Late May
Length of Walk:	3½ miles

The walk begins at the Deer Sanctuary Car Park where there is a large green. The route is downhill along a gravel path and part of the return journey is gently uphill.

You walk through plantations of pine, spruce, silver birch and beech. At the bottom of the gravel path is an old wooden footbridge which goes over a pretty stream. The location of the painting is only yards from the footbridge. In the left-hand background of the picture are some tall fir trees and since painting the scene, marks have been put on them which probably means they are due for felling. So, the painting will not be recognisable in the not too distant future. Other trees in the picture are oak and beech.

You will be lucky to see a muntjac as they are the least numerous type of deer in the Forest. However, the walk passes the Deer Sanctuary at Bolderwood so you are certain to see fallow deer there. Although the sanctuary is enclosed and you cannot go inside, deer are able to come and go using habitual places to creep under or jump. They can clear a six foot fence if pressed but prefer to pass under an obstacle or through a gap. The best time to visit is early afternoon when the keeper comes to feed them in the winter time.

When fawns are born in May/June bracken is a useful camouflage. Fawns spend many hours sleeping on their own whilst their mothers are grazing. They may look abandoned but mother is never far away and returns frequently to suckle her youngster. If you should be fortunate enough to come upon a fawn, resist the temptation to touch it — watch from a distance and then quietly steal away.

Beneath bracken grows one of Britain's rarest plants which only grows in the New Forest — the wild gladiolus — which has beautiful purpley-pink blooms. The gladiolus is protected by law and it is an offence to pick the blooms or dig up the plants. In fact, none of the flowers in the Forest should be picked because it is due to human damage over the years that so many wild flowers are disappearing.

One of the Commoners' rights which has fallen into disuse is the fern collection when bracken was harvested as litter for animals. The bracken could only be cut after 29th September when the fern's sap ceased to flow as earlier cutting would mean the plant bleeding to death. Gorse, or furze as it is called in the Forest, also came under this special right, and was used as feed. Another old right was that of holly cutting for the city traders for two weeks before Christmas. Heather too was once harvested in the autumn to make mats, skeps (baskets and beehives) and for the preparation of cosmetics.

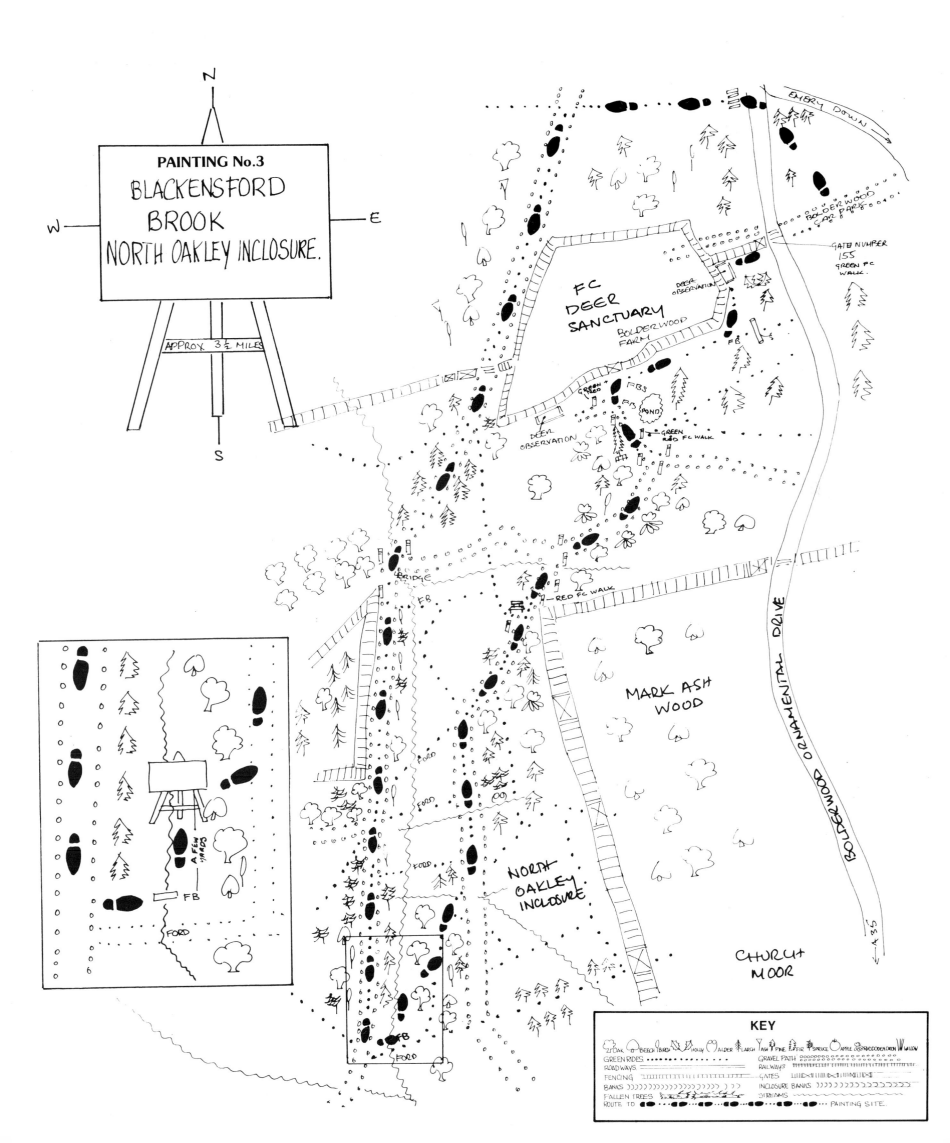

PAINTING No.3
BLACKENSFORD
BROOK
NORTH OAKLEY INCLOSURE.

APPROX 3½ MILES

N
W — E
S

EMBRY DOWN
BOLDERWOOD CAR PARK
GATE NUMBER 155 GREEN FC WALK.
FC DEER SANCTUARY
DEER OBSERVATION
BOLDERWOOD FARM
FB
GREEN FC RED
FB3
FB POND
DEER OBSERVATION
GREEN RED FC WALK
BRIDGE
FB
RED FC WALK
MARK ASH WOOD
BOLDERWOOD ORNAMENTAL DRIVE
A 35
FORD
FORD
FORD
NORTH OAKLEY INCLOSURE
CHURCH MOOR
FORD
FB
FORD

A FEW YARDS
FB
FORD

KEY

OAK BEECH BIRCH HOLLY ALDER LARCH ASH PINE FIR SPRUCE APPLE RHODODENDRON WILLOW

GREEN RIDES •••••••••••••••••••• GRAVEL PATH ∘∘∘∘∘∘∘∘∘∘∘∘∘
ROADWAYS ———————— RAILWAYS ⊥⊥⊥⊥⊥⊥⊥⊥⊥⊥⊥⊥⊥
FENCING ⊥⊥⊥⊥⊥⊥⊥⊥⊥⊥ GATES ⊐⊏⊐⊏⊐⊏⊐⊏
BANKS))))))))))))))) INCLOSURE BANKS)))))))))))))))
FALLEN TREES ✦✦✦✦✦✦✦ STREAMS ∼∼∼∼∼∼∼∼∼
ROUTE TO •••••••••••••• PAINTING SITE.

Dames Slough Inclosure, Burley

The delicate greens of May deepen as spring gives birth to summer. The heady and lovely scent of the hawthorn flower drifts on the breeze softening the serrated edges of life. Passing fallow deer, losing their winter coats, creamy white spots beginning to show through. Bracken grows high, straight and strong along the sides of crystal clear waters ever flowing towards the sea. Rhododendron bushes bloom. The flowers reflect an exciting flash of colour penetrating deep into the depths of the water mingling with the golds and browns of the gravel below. Tiny flying insects flitting back and forth. Trees high above cast shadows across the water. Sunlight brings blues and greys to the twinkling surface. Little lines of white foam bobbing and weaving through ripples made by water speeding over miniature rapids.

Dark liquid pools too deep to see the bottom.

Banks of golden sand and pale grey clay. Exposed tree roots weaving a pattern like giant lace. Last year's bracken festooning over and down into the water, a pretty shade of dark pink and light red to brown. Sunlight catching the green mosses, adding highlights to this spectacularly beautiful natural scene. I try to capture with paint on canvas this favoured little place, so well known to me it might be my own garden. To have a piece of my New Forest as my own is a joy to be denied me. Yet it all belongs to me, especially the streams. They are the eyes of the Forest bringing life to the landscape. How many eyes I wonder have they looked up into. How many eyes that have loved them as I do. How many other brown eyes, blue or green eyes? Now my eyes look lovingly into this stream when melancholy persists as I might into the eyes of someone I love and all sadness melts away.

COMMA BUTTERFLY.

PURPLE EMPEROR BUTTERFLY.

Dames Slough Inclosure
BURLEY

Painting No.4

PAINTING No.4

Place:	**DAMES SLOUGH INCLOSURE, BURLEY**
Time of Year:	Early June
Length of Walk:	2 miles

the rhododendrons, in one of the few places in the Forest where their beautiful blooms are reflected in water, are oak, ash and beech trees. There is a ford about 100 yards from the painting. The stream is called Blackensford one side of Dogkennel Bridge, then runs through Dames Slough, and in Vinney Ridge Inclosure becomes Blackwater.

Rhododendrons are only found in well defined areas of the Forest as they are prevented from spreading. Glorious though they are when in bloom, they are considered to be a weed and they serve no useful purpose. Nothing grows beneath them on the forest floor (conifer woods are the same) and in a working forest you could not have them covering too much land.

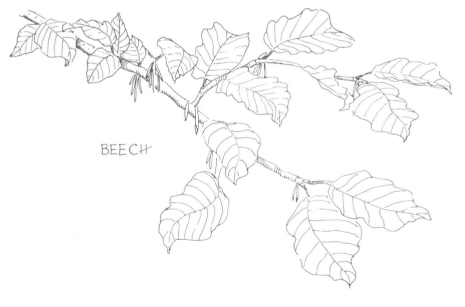

BEECH

The route shown is an easy walk along a gravel path and if wet it is advisable to return by the same path. The walk can be very muddy underfoot as the ride (a wide grassy path) gets churned up by the ridden horse. In winter it can be treacherous as the hoof holes in the ground fill up with water and then freeze. It is not a good idea to take a dog unless he is well controlled or on a lead as main roads are nearby.

Part of the walk follows a stream which is edged with small spruce conifers, the type we think of as Christmas trees. Around

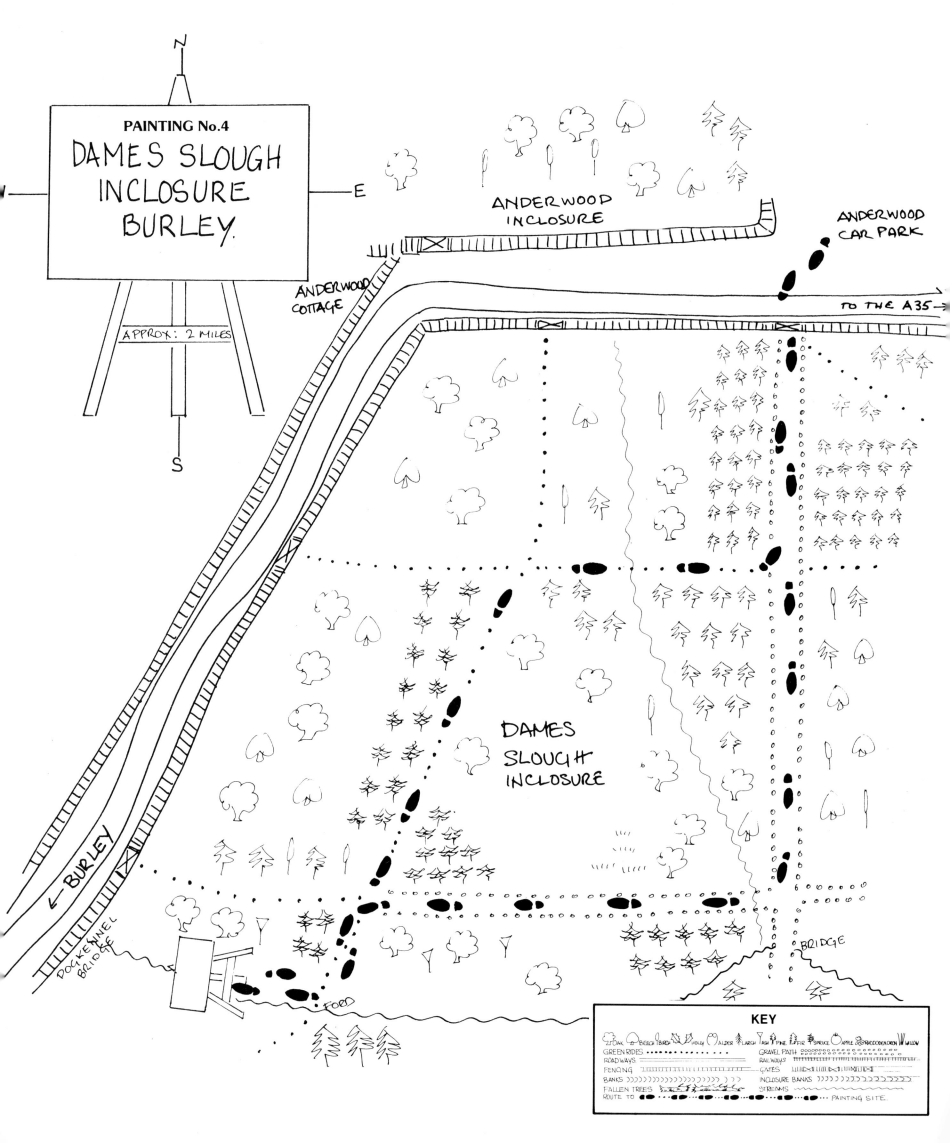

PAINTING No.4

DAMES SLOUGH INCLOSURE BURLEY.

N

E

S

APPROX: 2 MILES

ANDERWOOD INCLOSURE

ANDERWOOD CAR PARK

ANDERWOOD COTTAGE

TO THE A35

← BURLEY

DOCKENNEL BRIDGE

DAMES SLOUGH INCLOSURE

FORD

BRIDGE

KEY

OAK   BEECH   BIRCH   HOLLY   ALDER   LARCH   ASH   PINE   FIR   SPRUCE   APPLE   RHODODENDRON   WILLOW

GREEN RIDES ··········   GRAVEL PATH ooooooooo

ROADWAYS ────────   RAILWAYS ╫╫╫╫╫╫╫╫╫

FENCING ‖‖‖‖‖‖‖   GATES ‖‖‖⊠‖‖‖

BANKS ⟩⟩⟩⟩⟩⟩⟩⟩   INCLOSURE BANKS ⟩⟩⟩⟩⟩⟩⟩⟩

FALLEN TREES ▰▰▰▰   STREAMS ∼∼∼∼∼

ROUTE TO ●●●●●●●●●●●●   PAINTING SITE.

Summer's Song

Sky larks singing from a hovering position high in the sky. The 'peeoo' call of buzzards overhead. The rasping sound of the Dartford Warbler shouting a warning when you get too near the young they're still feeding. The buzzing of a nest of wild bees. These are the sounds of summer.

Being able to paint fifteen hours a day non-stop. Picking insects off the paint. The smell of rain just before it falls and the scent of honeysuckle. Strong greens of summer, blue skies with fluffy clouds peeping through beech trees. Oak leaves changing from yellow ochre of spring to their summer coat. Being dive bombed by a curlew. A cooling shower of rain, a godsend on a long hot summer walk.

Fallow bucks with antlers in velvet and in golden summer pelage. Always hoping to come across a rutting roe deer. The sight of fallow fawns playing and chasing in and out of the green bracken.

Rhododendrons in full bloom. Laying flat on Wilverley Plain to look at the tiny world of flowers there. Meadow browns fluttering over a grassy ride. The beautiful dog roses, crab apples forming.

The peace of all these things is summer in my New Forest.

THE DOG ROSE

47

Little Stubby Hat, near Bartley

Hazel's hand was stretched out behind her, the palm open towards me. She had seen something. At a whispered command our dogs sat. Hazel was on her knees, looking up the gravel path we were about to cross, binoculars to her eyes. I crept towards her. I raised my glasses to look and there on the path, warming itself in the summer sun, eyes closed, golden red fur gleaming in the bright light, was a beautiful young fox.

After a long watch we decided to go on and cross the gravel path. Once the other side we couldn't resist watching a little longer. All of a sudden he scratched, stretched and came trotting along the path towards us. We couldn't move now or we would be seen. We lay as flat to the ground as we could, holding the dogs down with us. The wind coming from behind him, he was totally unaware of our presence. Just at the point when all was about to be revealed, he turned onto a track taking him away from us.

Such a pleasure to see and enjoy without being seen. I wish I could share this kind of experience with those who only see the fox as a vicious verminous creature. Yes, the fox is a killer but usually only for food.

For years I have 'sat on the fence' about fox hunting. I have listened to the arguments from both sides. The huntsmen say foxes need to be controlled. Hunting is less cruel than gassing or trapping. The fox dies or gets away. Those against ask, if that's the case, why are foxes conserved for the hunt and in some areas even bred in captivity to be released in front of the hounds? And why are badger sett holes blocked with earth to prevent a fox 'going to ground'? And why, when a fox does hide in a hole, do they have to send terriers down after him equipped with electronic devices? The terrier-men spend hours digging him out for the hounds to tear to pieces, or to quote the hunter's jargon, "Break him up boys."

Some farmers maintain the fox will kill lambs and chickens; others say protect your chickens properly; and most welcome the fox to keep down rabbits and rats. Experts say the fox will not kill a lamb but will take off any stillborn or dead one. No fox brought up on rabbits will kill chickens and vice versa. And so the battle goes on.

It seems ironic to fox-watch in this area. Only a few hundred yards from this painting is the New Forest Foxhound Kennels. But then, the one we saw

  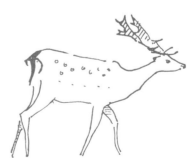 

was too young to know the fox cub hunting season was almost upon him.

Nearby Little Stubby Hat is Gutter Heath. The New Forest has many lovely open heathlands. If you can find time to visit one of them you may see, as I did on a fine day in July, hundreds of tiny blue butterflies constantly fluttering over bell heather. The flowers' subtle, delicate tones of pink and purple mixing with green foliage and brown peat. Making a swirling sea of colour, rippling with life and shimmering in the sunshine.

Glistening jewels of light flashed as the gentle breeze on my face tore like a raging wind through a spider's web. Many legs coming from under a fluorescent green body weaving back and forth, drawing two stalks of heather closer and closer together. A mating pair of silver-studded blue butterflies became caught in the spider's carefully placed net. They struggled to be free without letting one another go. The watching human, with one finger, released the lovers from the perilous trap. Unaware of the danger I represented, they obviously sank their whole existence into the ecstasies of making love.

A silver-studded lady, dressed in mink brown and orange spots, sat head downwards on a pink flower. Bottom end up, she twisted and turned her back wings like the hips of a belly dancer to attract a mate. One descended and landed upon her. As they touched, her wings quivered at such a speed only a blur could be seen. He flew away apparently rejected.

Dozens of little blue males searched the short heather for a responsive female. Blue to the eye but in fact not blue at all. Minute scales reflecting the only colour of the spectrum not absorbed into the wings. Blue.

PAINTING No.5

Place:	**LITTLE STUBBY HAT, NEAR BARTLEY**
Time of Year:	**July**
Length of Walk:	**3 miles**

the first occasion Monica and Hazel visited this spot, they had lunch here and were harrassed by a pair of furious wrens. Realising they were sitting close to the nest, they were forced to get up and move!

Disused badger setts are used as lairs by foxes, and particularly when they 'go to ground' if hunted. Cubs are born in April and a vixen, who can have as many as six offspring, takes them out with her to learn to hunt when they are about a month old. Their diet is mainly rabbits, but they do eat rats, mice, squirrel, frogs, partridges, pheasants etc. and even hedgehogs and beetles. You can tell when a fox has killed a bird as he bites off the feathers whereas some birds of prey pluck them. Foxes will skin a hedgehog unlike a badger who also eats them but consumes every part. The best time to watch foxes is in the early evening although it is not uncommon to see them abroad during the day.

Fox hunting in the New Forest takes place twice a week from August to April.

This walk is flat but it is not advisable to do it on a very hot day because the gravel path reflects the heat. In places, the stream is very bendy and deep, passing through areas where old trees have fallen. It is a quiet place and can be wet underfoot between the first footbridge (after the second gate) and Nicholas Corner. On

Anne with Eric Ashby's vixen, Sheba, at his wildlife sanctuary in the Forest.

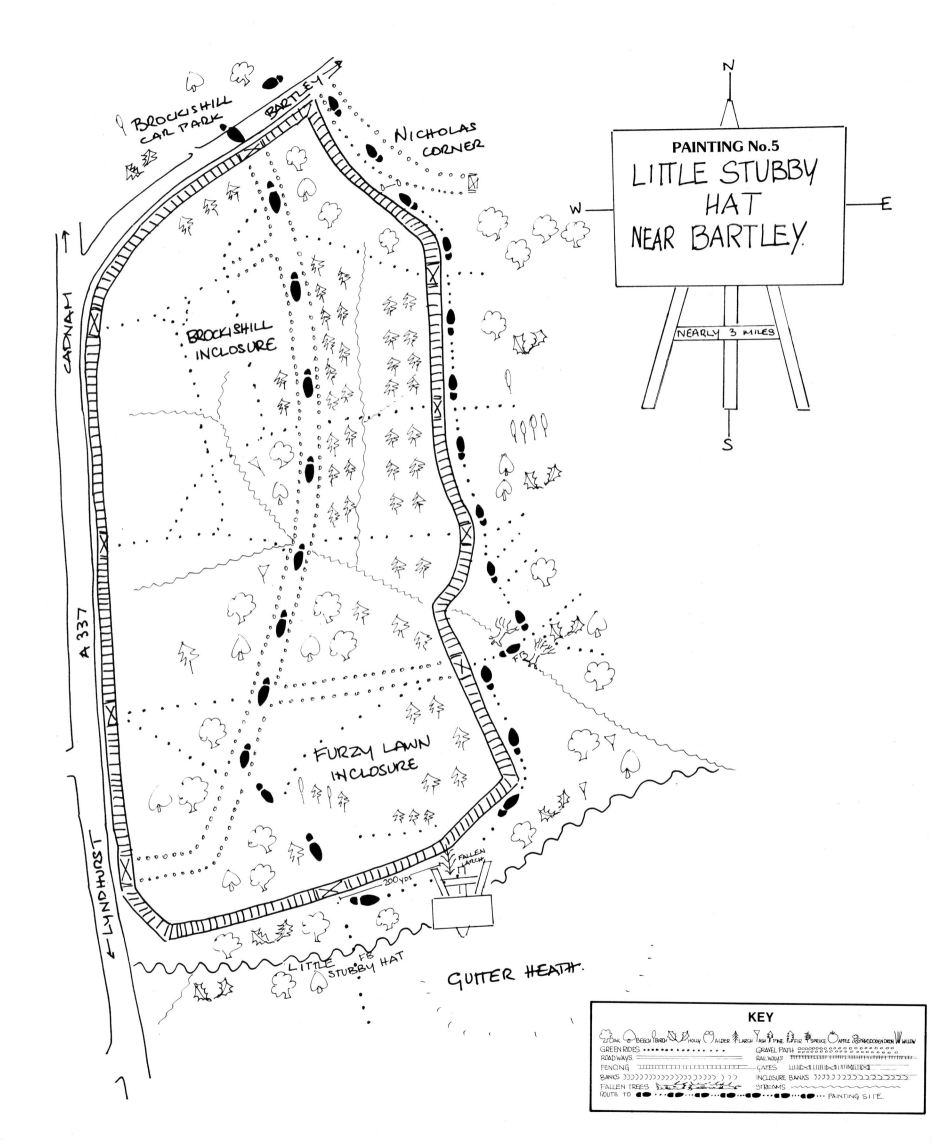

PAINTING No.5

LITTLE STUBBY HAT NEAR BARTLEY.

NEARLY 3 MILES

BROCKISHILL CAR PARK

BARTLEY

NICHOLAS CORNER

CADNAM

A 337

LYNDHURST

BROCKISHILL INCLOSURE

FURZY LAWN INCLOSURE

FB

200 YDS

FALLEN LARCH

FB

LITTLE STUBBY HAT

GUTTER HEATH.

KEY

OAK   BEECH   BIRCH   HOLLY   ALDER   LARCH   ASH   PINE   FIR   SPRUCE   APPLE   RHODODENDRON   WILLOW

GREEN RIDES ....   GRAVEL PATH ooooooooooooo

ROADWAYS ════════════   RAILWAYS ┼┼┼┼┼┼┼┼┼┼

FENCING ⊥⊥⊥⊥⊥⊥⊥⊥⊥⊥⊥   GATES ⊔⊐⊏⊐⊏⊐

BANKS)))))))))))))   INCLOSURE BANKS))))))))))))

FALLEN TREES   STREAMS ∿∿∿∿∿∿∿∿

ROUTE TO ●●● •••••• ●●● ••• PAINTING SITE.

Little Stubby Hat
NEAR BARTLEY

Painting No.5

RED FOX

Dockens Water
MOYLES COURT

Painting No.6

Dockens Water, Moyles Court

Rain was pouring down on the Friday, so I wasn't worried. It'll be cancelled I thought. But the next morning I opened my eyes to brilliant sunlight. Fear hit me. Suddenly I felt terribly ill.

'I can't do it. Thelma you'll have to phone up and tell them I can't do it. I'm ill.'

'It's only nerves, you'll be alright once you start painting.'

'No, I'm ill, I tell you. I've got flu or something worse!'

Thelma sympathised but ignored me. Feeling like last year's warmed-up Christmas pudding, I drove my battered old Daf to Moyles Court. Today we were filming my part in the B.B.C. television series 'The New Foresters'. Arriving half an hour before the arranged time, I was horrified to find THEY were all there. How would I ever get through the day? A familiar face appeared, all smiles and pride. Good old Norman Chislett, he'd come to cheer me on. He and I were members of a local target shooting club. Now I had to smile, put on a brave face. Couldn't let the side down. Thelma and Norman positioned themselves 'off set' to watch this poor sick person make a complete idiot of herself!

Cindy, my dog, was about ten years old then and full of life. Dockens Water was her favourite place. She would spend many happy hours gathering stones, with head completely under water for ages. Today, her antics were just what the cameraman, David Bowerman, wanted. I was upstaged by my own dog!

Just as I was getting into my stride painting I was told that David made films with an artist who regularly appeared on television. This man filming me was used to working with a 'proper' artist. Panic set in again.

Interviewer Dennis Skillicorn had never worked on television before, this was his first series and I was the first one to be filmed. I had been on television a few years before — suddenly I was the old hand!

I had from 10 a.m. to 1 p.m. to complete the painting. I'm still not sure how I did it.

We broke for a pub lunch and the rest of the team became individuals. The young lady with the clipboard was Steve Evans (Assistant to the Producer). Soundman, Martin Dale knew Thelma's son.

Later, Dennis, Martin and I set off to find a quiet place to record some 'talk-over'. I took them up a gravel lane that leads to a little church at Stuckton. Normally a quiet place, one car after another came along. Starting and stopping several times, we eventually 'got it in the can'.

Next stop Fordingbridge where my work was on exhibition. A glass of sherry with my lunch and my skin had turned from green to pink. My nose has a tendency to go red when alcohol has been that close to it, but outside broadcasts don't have make-up departments, so I had to go on, beacon and all.

Dennis and I had to come over a bridge and cross the road into the exhibition. Just as we're about to cross, a fire engine roared over the bridge. Cut! Try again. Car comes along and stops right in the middle of it all. Cut! Back we go, wait for the signal and . . . quick, quick, slow. Here we come again. Chatting away we reach the edge of the pavement. One car, two cars, three. Cut! Patience didn't run out. Everyone was seeing the funny side of it. One more time. Cut! The soundman can't hear Dennis. Only I was wearing a microphone and Dennis needed to be closer to it. We came over the bridge for the fifth time thinking we must look as if Dennis had my arm in a hammerlock. We seemed twisted together! But the end product was simply wonderful. I will always be grateful to that small band of highly skilled people, including those I never met who edited out all those mistakes. Saturday, 2nd August, 1980 is one day I will never forget.

PAINTING No.6

Place: **DOCKENS WATER, MOYLES COURT**

Time of Year: **Late June**

There is no real car park at Dockens Water and everyone parks by the water splash. In summer, and often during other months, an ice cream man comes to this spot.

Being such a special place for Monica and her old dog, Cindy, she frequently paints at this spot and the scene in the picture is only a few yards from the car. In their home-decorating days, Monica and Thelma often came here in the dark at the end of a long day to walk Cindy.

There are always ponies around this area and it is a dangerous place to pet them. Visitors to the New Forest are requested not to feed any animals as this is illegal and incurs a £20 fine. Feeding encourages them to go onto the roads and on average 140 ponies and cattle are killed every year in traffic accidents, mainly in places where people break the law and feed animals beside the road. Many ponies are hit and hurt, the accident not being reported, and die from injuries later.

Ponies and other animals can also die from discarded rubbish. Being inquisitive, it has been known for a pony to sniff at a plastic bag and suck it into his windpipe, suffocating the poor animal. Others have died when their intestines have become strangled by plastic string and other debris. Apart from the fact that litter spoils the look of the Forest, it does untold damage — broken glass can easily cause a forest fire — so please take yours home with you if there is no bin nearby.

All the commonable animals, including around 3,000 ponies, 40 donkeys and 2,000 cattle, have to be branded by law and each Commoner has his own brand. Horses are branded at the annual drift, usually on the shoulder, and these brands can be clearly seen in the summer when the ponies have lost their shaggy winter coat. Brands are essential in identifying animals involved in accidents.

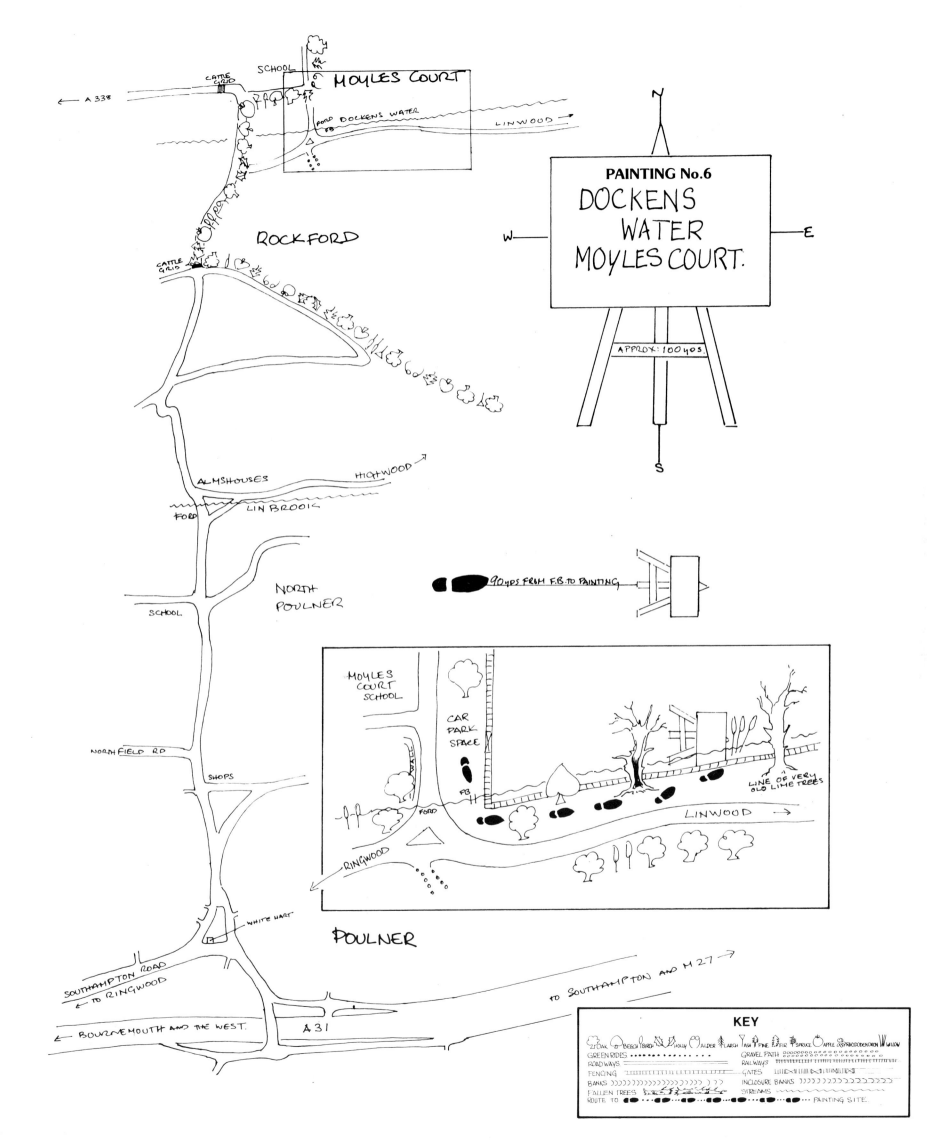

A 338

CATTLE GRID

SCHOOL

MOYLES COURT

FORD DOCKENS WATER
F.B

LINWOOD

ROCKFORD

CATTLE GRID

PAINTING No.6

DOCKENS
WATER
MOYLES COURT.

N

W

E

S

APPROX: 100 YDS

ALMSHOUSES

HIGHWOOD

FORD

LIN BROOK

90 YDS FROM F.B. TO PAINTING

NORTH
POULNER

SCHOOL

MOYLES
COURT
SCHOOL

CAR
PARK
SPACE

NORTHFIELD RD

SHOPS

FORD

FB

LINE OF VERY
OLD LIME TREES

LINWOOD

RINGWOOD

WHITE HART

POULNER

SOUTHAMPTON ROAD
← TO RINGWOOD

TO SOUTHAMPTON AND M 27 →

← BOURNEMOUTH AND THE WEST.

A 31

KEY

OAK BEECH BIRCH HOLLY ALDER LARCH ASH PINE FIR SPRUCE APPLE RHODODENDRON WILLOW

GREEN RIDES ●●●●●●●●●● GRAVEL PATH ○○○○○○○○○○

ROADWAYS RAILWAYS

FENCING GATES

BANKS INCLOSURE BANKS

FALLEN TREES STREAMS ～～～～～

ROUTE TO ●●●●● PAINTING SITE.

TAWNY OWL

Latchmore Brook, Fritham

Oh! My God, what's that?" Hazel was running ahead calling the dogs. Sika came to me shaking her head. She had two little holes on each side of her nose. I squeezed them to make them bleed. No words that I write here could convey the fear that flowed through me at that moment. Within seconds Sika became subdued, trying to curl up on dried bracken and lie down. Her nose began to swell.

It was a hot April day. The sort of weather an adder loves when he lies and basks in the sunshine. He only strikes in self-defence and the thing we had always feared had happened. An adder had struck out at Sika.

We knew we had a three mile walk back to the car. Stifling panic we steadily retraced our steps. Sika was doing well. The heat was intense. Huze went on faster back to the car while Sika and I made our way straight ahead towards the road. From the top of the hill I could see that the road was at least another mile. Sika obviously had a headache. I felt sick expecting her to collapse. The last leg of our journey was uphill so I let her cool off in the stream. She was reluctant to go on.

Coaxing and cajoling, I urged her on. We reached the road as Haze arrived with the car. We rushed into Fordingbridge to the Police Station, only to find it closed. Well, it was lunchtime! I ran back to a lady walking along.

"Park Road," she said with a rich Welsh accent. "There's a vet in Park Road."

We were lucky, a lovely man opened his surgery and gave Sika treatment. We took her home and prayed she would be alright. For the next twenty hours Thelma and I fussed over her. By then it was morning. Bruising and swelling made her unrecognisable. We took her to our own vet at West Moors for more medication. He told us the main worry was damage to the heart so she must be kept quiet for several days. With so much poison and drugs in her we were to find that no problem.

Adder bites are very painful and Sika had been bitten both sides of her nose, so it was no wonder she was having a bad time. She slept a lot but her appetite was unimpaired. Forty-eight hours and several Bonio's later, the turning point came. The monster face was beginning to subside and Sika's was coming back. She was going to be alright.

The one good thing to come from that nightmare is that I now have tablets to carry in case, God forbid, it should ever happen again. There is no miracle cure and another bite would mean being ill but at least the tablets will help until a vet can be seen. So be warned, if you are going to walk in the Forest regularly, seek your vet's advice before your dog feels the red hot business-end of an adder.

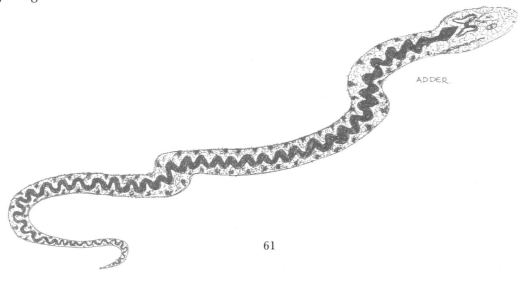

ADDER.

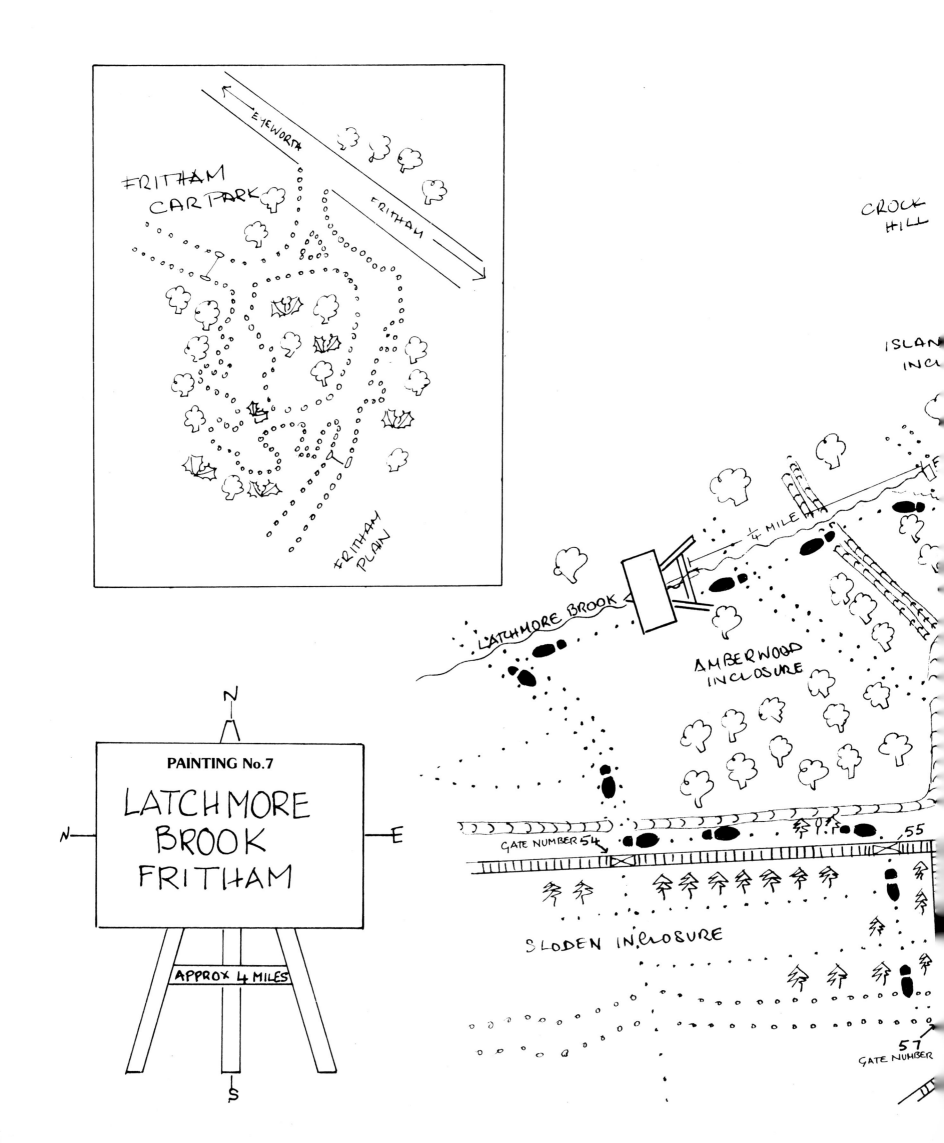

FRITHAM CAR PARK

EYEWORTH

FRITHAM

FRITHAM PLAN

CROCK HILL

ISLAN
INCL

LATCHMORE BROOK

¼ MILE

AMBERWOOD INCLOSURE

GATE NUMBER 54

55

SLODEN INCLOSURE

57
GATE NUMBER

N

N   E

S

PAINTING No.7

LATCHMORE
BROOK
FRITHAM

APPROX 4 MILES

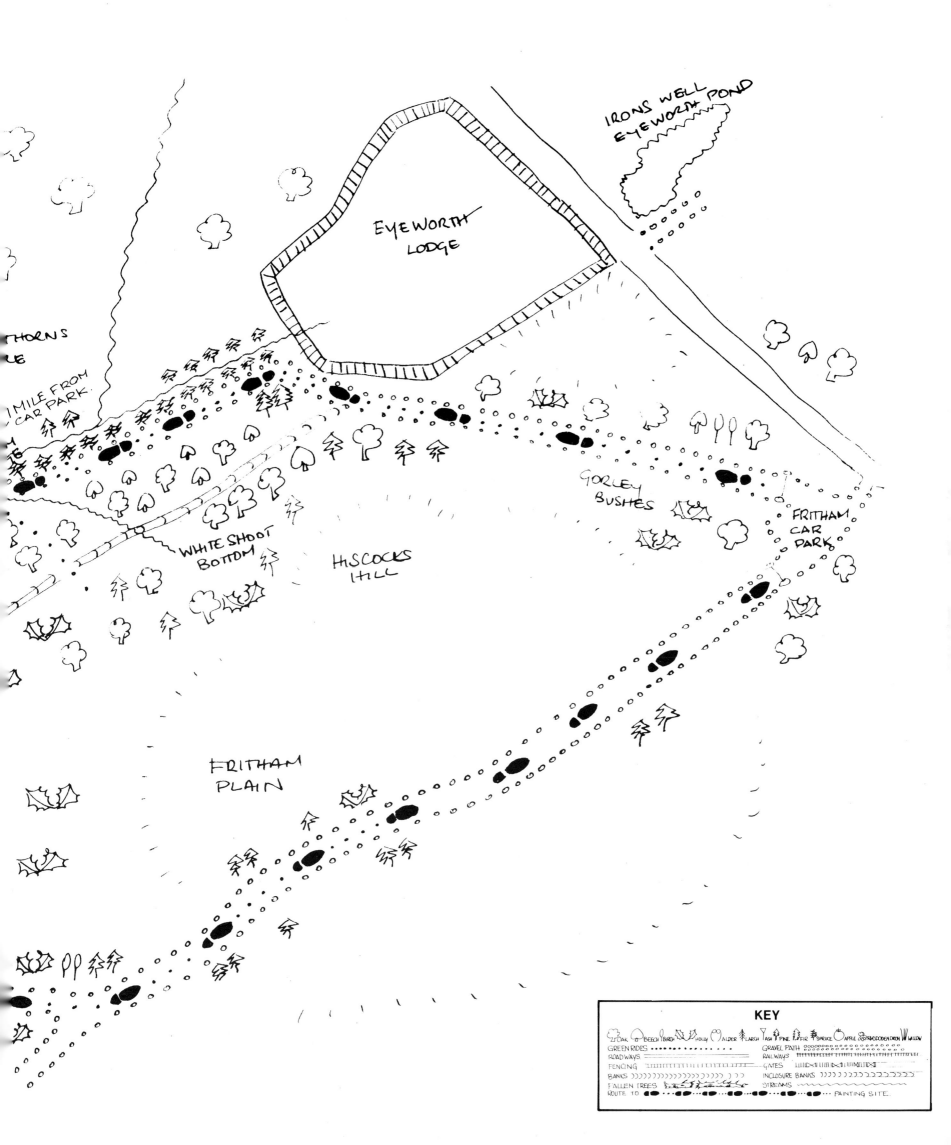

IRONS WELL
EYEWORTH POND

EYEWORTH
LODGE

THORNS
LE

1 MILE FROM
CAR PARK.

TO

GORLEY
BUSHES

FRITHAM
CAR
PARK

WHITE SHOOT
BOTTOM

HISCOCKS
HILL

FRITHAM
PLAIN

KEY

Oak Beech Birch Holly Alder Larch Ash Pine Fir Spruce Apple Rhododendron Willow

GREEN RIDES .... GRAVEL PATH ooooooooooooooooo

ROADWAYS ═══════════════ RAILWAYS ┼┼┼┼┼┼┼┼┼┼┼┼┼┼┼┼┼

FENCING ⊥⊥⊥⊥⊥⊥⊥⊥⊥⊥⊥⊥⊥ GATES ⊥⊥⊥⊥⊥⊥⊥⊥⊥⊥

BANKS ﻬﻬﻬﻬﻬﻬﻬﻬﻬﻬﻬﻬﻬ INCLOSURE BANKS ﻬﻬﻬﻬﻬﻬﻬﻬﻬﻬﻬﻬﻬﻬﻬ

FALLEN TREES ⟋⟍⟋⟍⟋⟍ STREAMS ∿∿∿∿∿∿

ROUTE TO ●○●○●○●○●○●○●○●○●○ PAINTING SITE.

PAINTING No.7

Place: **LATCHMORE BROOK, FRITHAM**
Time of Year: Late August
Length of Walk: 4 miles

This is probably the most difficult walk in the book and it goes through an area which Monica feels is more the deepest heart of the Forest than anywhere else. The walk begins easily enough with a down-hill gravel path. From Fritham Bridge it goes along the side of a brook. The first half of the walk back is uphill until you arrive (out of breath!) at a gravel path which is followed for more than a mile back to the car park. This path crosses the open expanse of Fritham Plain which is boiling hot in summer, freezing in winter and nearly always windy.

A word of warning about Fritham car park: this is a favourite spot for professional robbers who have keys for picking car locks. Monica leaves her binoculars and camera cases open so the empty insides can be seen from the window.

Lots of animal tracks criss-cross the path in parts of this area. Hidden deep within the dark woods are the earth burrows full of tunnels called badger earths or setts, where badgers retreat during the day. Usually a sett has several entrances and outside the main one will be a pile of old bracken, sometimes mixed with bluebells, which has been pulled out from the sleeping chamber. A sort of regular clean sheets habit!

Badgers have cubs, any number from one to six, in February and the cubs stay with their parents until at least the autumn. They have scent glands which they use to find their way about and mark territorial boundaries. Nearby the sett will be a scratching tree and a latrine or pit, for badgers are great creatures of habit. To find a pit doesn't necessarily mean that a sett is nearby because badgers have "public loos" which they use when out on night hunting trips.

Monica and Sika's frightening experience with the adder is

not, thankfully, a common one. The adder is Britain's only venomous snake and is easily recognised by zig-zag markings along its back. They are normally ultra-sensitive to vibrations in the ground and will quickly slither away into the undergrowth at the sound of footfalls. Warm weather is the most usual time to see them as they like to coil up and bask in the sun. Their natural reaction to being taken unawares is to strike out in self-defence.

If you should be unlucky enough to be bitten by an adder, do not panic. Keep calm, wash the area with clean water, do not cut or attempt to suck the poison out of the wound, and go to a hospital at once. If your dog gets bitten, prompt action is essential as the poison can affect a dog far more quickly than a human. Get to a vet as soon as possible.

There are two other snakes to be found in the Forest but neither are poisonous. One is the grass snake, which is much bigger than an adder and has a prominent yellow collar. The other is the rare smooth snake which has twin rows of small dark spots along its back. It kills its prey by suffocation using its coils like a boa constrictor. Sometimes snakes can be seen swimming in the streams.

All these snakes can be seen behind the safety of low walls at the Holidays Hill Reptiliary, just north of the A35, two miles west of Lyndhurst. Here every species of reptile to be found in the Forest is kept including the rare sand lizard. There are also all three species of British newts, toads, frogs, common lizards (who have living young) and the legless lizard known as the slow worm.

A New Forest character connected with the snakes was famous 'Brusher' Mills, the snake-catcher. Born and bred in the Forest, he rejected ordinary life and lived for twenty-one years in the Forest sheltered by a cone-shaped hut built of turf and branches. He received his nickname through brushing the local cricket pitch and became a celebrity by demonstrating his prowess in handling snakes. He carried snakes around in two tins slung around his shoulders and showed interested people how he could immobilise them. He used a long-handled fork to catch the snake and scissors to extract the venom. It is said he caught 4,000 adders and 30,000 other species of snake in his lifetime. In 1905 he died after being evicted from his beloved hut by the Crown Authorities who burnt it down.

Latchmore Brook
FRITHAM

65

Autumn Colours

Sometimes as early as September the green of the oak trees turns to yellow ochre preparing us for the colours to come. October tries to hang on to summer but never succeeds. The first two weeks in November are usually the most dramatic for colour completely dominated by autumn.

Once more the beech tree is the most beautiful. Now it is reds and golds that the sun can shine right through. Falling leaves at first mingle with the earth browns and moss greens weaving a colourful carpet to cover the forest floor. Molinia grass a bright fawn under Douglas Fir and Scots Pine at Rhinefield, one of the most beautiful areas to be during autumn. As more and more leaves float to the ground like huge golden snow flakes, so the carpet pile deepens.

Highland Water is probably the loveliest stream of all this time of the year. A wide stream, sometimes very deep, it runs from Withybed Bottom on by Woolsmoor Meads, under Millyford Bridge and the Roman arch and through Queen's Bower, picking up Bagshot Gutter, Blackwater, Warwickslade Cutting and Ober Water on its way. From Bolderford Bridge it goes out to sea via Brockenhurst as the Lymington River. To walk along its banks at Holidays Hill when leaves make thick patterns and ever moving shapes on the surface of the water; when the sun's rays crash through gently swaying branches, shining down and spotlighting leaves picked up by the breeze looking like ballet dancers on a massive stage is the nearest to heaven I am ever likely to get.

67

PAINTING No.8

Place: Dockens Bridge, near Rockford

Time of Year: November

History surrounds this area of the New Forest. Nearby is Moyles Court, now a school but once the home of Dame Alicia Lisle, who was accused of harbouring two rebels there after the Battle of Sedgemoor. She was tried by the notorious Judge Jeffreys and sentenced to be burned alive. A stay of execution was obtained and King James II was petitioned for clemency. The King showed little mercy and seventy year old Dame Alicia was beheaded at Winchester in 1685. She was buried in Ellingham Churchyard and local tradition has it that her ghost drives from there in a wagon with headless horses and no driver across Dockens Bridge and back to her home at Moyles Court.

Today, Monica worries about the number of heavy lorries which rumble over the old bridge. One day it will probably have to go. In recent years many of the silver birch have become old and dangerous and have been felled. No-one has done anything about replacing them yet.

It saddens her that people are not aware that we need trees far more than they need us. They clean the very air we breathe and shelter us from high winds. Ringwood (where she lives) she enlikens to a wind tunnel because so many trees have been cut down to make room for the town's growth and to get rid of the problem of leaves on gardens. Nature, fortunately, doesn't have the gardener's tidy mind.

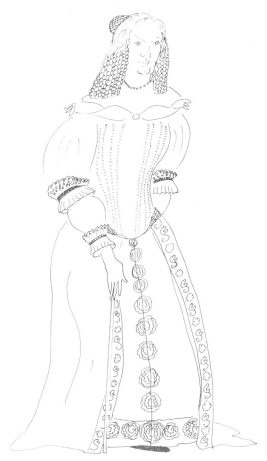

DAME ALICIA LISLE

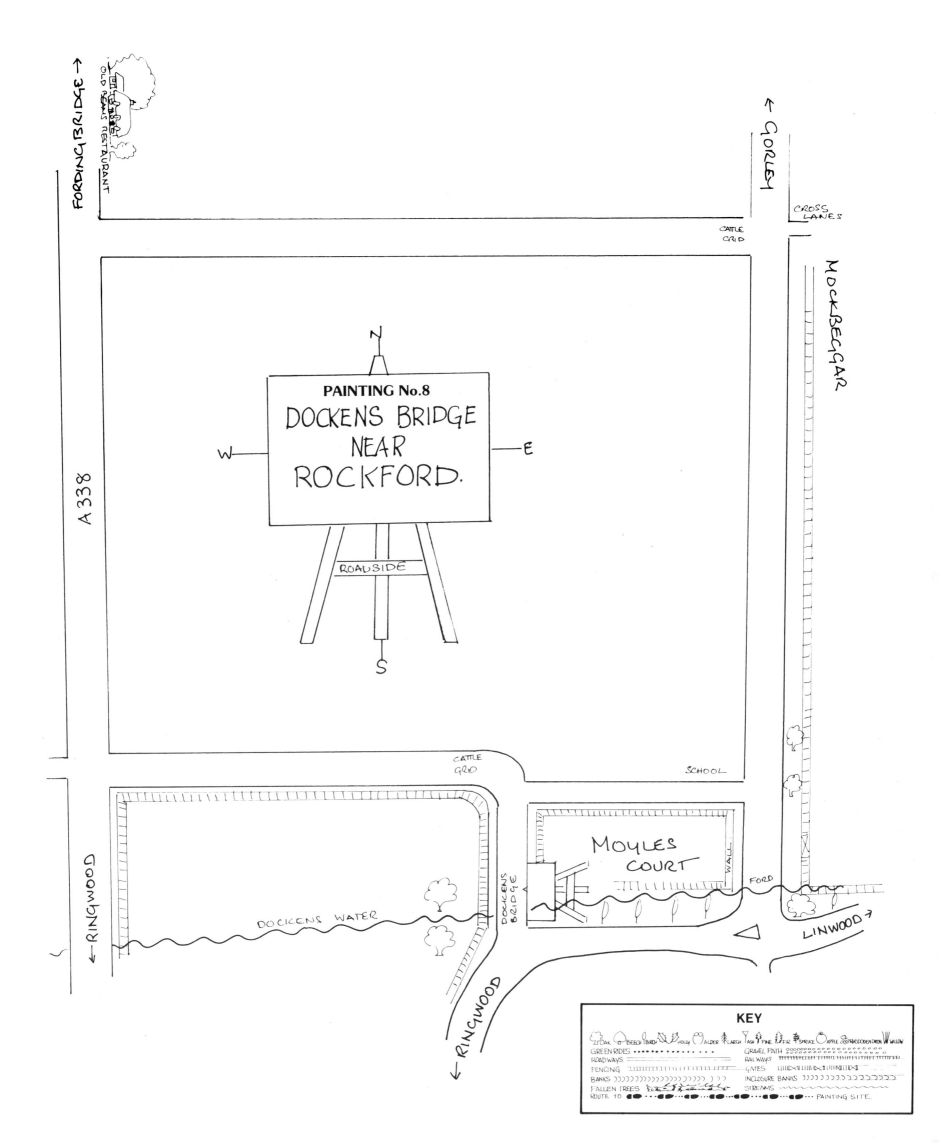

FORDINGBRIDGE →

OLD BEAMS RESTAURANT

← GORLEY

CROSS LANES

CATTLE GRID

MOCKBEGGAR

A 338

N

PAINTING No.8

DOCKENS BRIDGE
NEAR
ROCKFORD.

W

E

ROADSIDE

S

CATTLE GRID

SCHOOL

← RINGWOOD

DOCKENS WATER

DOCKENS BRIDGE

MOYLES COURT

WALL

FORD

LINWOOD →

← RINGWOOD

KEY

OAK BEECH BIRCH HOLLY ALDER LARCH ASH PINE FIR SPRUCE APPLE CHESTNUT RHODODENDRON WILLOW

GREEN RIDES •••••••••••• GRAVEL PATH ∘∘∘∘∘∘∘∘∘∘
ROADWAYS ═══════════ RAILWAYS ┼┼┼┼┼┼┼┼┼┼┼┼┼
FENCING ┬┬┬┬┬┬┬┬┬┬ GATES ⊏⊐⊏⊐⊏⊐
BANKS ⟩⟩⟩⟩⟩⟩⟩⟩⟩⟩ INCLOSURE BANKS ⟩⟩⟩⟩⟩⟩⟩⟩⟩⟩
FALLEN TREES ⊱⊰⊱⊰ STREAMS ∿∿∿∿∿∿∿
ROUTE TO •●•●•●•●•●•●•●•●•● PAINTING SITE.

Dockens Bridge, near Rockford

Early morning sunshine, not yet strong enough to warm the air, lighting the bridge as if a spotlight had been turned on. A moment ago greys and browns were creating its shape on the canvas. Now suddenly red, orange, pink, green, blue. I could see the underside of the bridge, light reflecting up from the water flowing beneath it showing me almost a different shape. I was painting an old friend. Many times before I had painted here, from the bank above or more often with the legs of my easel in the water, my feet too sometimes. Cindy's feet were always in the stream and this day was no exception. She gathered stones as usual, while I struggled with colour, cursing my own inadequacy.

Several hours passed peacefully by. The sun was now very warm on my back. A quiet road this time of year, just a few people taking the pretty way to work. A tractor passed with a nod from its driver. Someone out for a morning horse ride, 'Good morning, lovely day!'

I was completely relaxed now. The painting was appearing in front of me just like those books you have as a kid. You put water on the page and a picture is there as if by magic. It doesn't always happen that way but THIS was one of THOSE days. Nature was changing coats. Rich golds and browns replacing the yellows and greens. My knife seemed to slip into overdrive.

'Wow, hey look!' Car doors were slamming. I could hear running feet. I turned to look. Behind me a car was parked from which came a young man, excited, gesticulating. He couldn't believe his luck! He and his friends, still sitting in the car, had seen the programme 'The New Foresters' on television. They liked it so much that a pact had been made to find the very place. They had driven down from London that morning and someone in Fordingbridge had directed them here. They thought they were dreaming to find me standing there painting!

Of course, I told them the story. Cindy and I took the young people to the actual spot where the film was made. Their excitement was touching. Such is the power of television. Perhaps I'm wrong but, to this day, although not trying to spoil enthusiasm, I feel compelled to impress upon people that it's only me. Just an ageing country woman with a God-given ability to produce something that people like enough to buy therefore enabling me to make a living doing a job I love.

The New Forest is my life. Every aspect of it touches me, from trying not to step on a 'motorway' made by wood ants crossing a path, to watching the skill of a woodsman felling a tree.

Dockens Bridge
NEAR ROCKFORD

71

Painting No.8

Anses Wood
NEAR CADMANS POOL

Painting No.9

WESSEX SADDLEBACK

Anses Wood, near Cadmans Pool

Tracks much bigger and wider than any made by a fallow or roe deer. Red perhaps? Cindy found droppings nearby that fitted the description of a red stag during the rutting season and this was the right time. The tracks were carefully measured, then followed. Just a minute! We've been caught like this before. Last time we stalked a deer with feet this size it led us straight to a herd of cattle. But these looked too small for a calf.

Thelma was with me on this day and it was she who saw Cindy's tail wagging behind a bush. We ran over to find her having a friendly chat with a very pregnant black and white pig. The sow's belly touched the ground as she waddled slowly along, her well-equipped nose ploughing through the surface layer of leaves and peat. Cindy walked with her, sniffing to see what was so interesting.

Pigs will often be found at Fritham running around the lawns by the car park. Sika, my black labrador, was spell-bound on her first encounter with them there. That was on a late summer's day while out walking with Haze when we stopped to rest on a seat. It was so hot even Sally, Haze's dog, was lying flat out. Sika was just dozing off on my de-booted feet.

A little white nose appeared. Then eyes followed by ears. The eyes were looking curiously at the sleeping black monster. A floppy ear twitched as the little nose sniffed so close it almost touched. Sika opened one eye and immediately shot up in the air. All four feet off the ground. The little piglet fled screaming back into the undergrowth.

A few minutes later the nose re-appeared, backed up this time by half a dozen slightly larger ones. With necks outstretched, they approached Sika like a line of soldiers. Sika sat down, then stood up, not quite sure what to do. She took a couple of steps back. Sally, being older and much wiser, completely ignored the whole thing. Another dozen infantry pigs fell in. A dirty-legged front line gained confidence led by a completely mud-covered and tiny general. The troops pushed forward like a little army of white chessmen and they closed ranks around the black queen, Sika. She looked around at us as if to say 'What shall I do?' She decided to offer them a friendly nose to sniff.

Just at that moment someone in the back row saw mum. With a screech of delight he took off at speed like a bucking bronco. With that the rest of the army deserted, kicking up their heels and squealing while a slightly bemused dog and two very amused women looked on.

PAINTING No.9

Place:	**ANSES WOOD, NEAR CADMANS POOL**
Time of Year:	**November**
Length of Walk:	**1½ miles**

Cadmans Pool where this walk begins is near Stoney Cross which became a household word in 1986 when the hippy convoy camped there after being evicted from Stonehenge.

This is not an easy walk if it is wet underfoot. On the way back, the last 200 yards of the path is difficult to follow because there are lots of animal tracks. Stick to the main one and this will bring you uphill back to the car park. The walk is best done in summer because the stream often floods its banks.

Cadmans Pool is a pleasant place to sit and watch damsel-flies and dragon-flies skimming across the water. They are just some of the hundreds of insects to be seen in the Forest. In summer there are quite a number of stinging flies, mosquitoes and midges which make life miserable for animal watchers. As compensation there are lots of species of beautiful butterflies including the silver spotted blue and meadow browns.

Pigs are often seen in the Forest, particularly in September, October or November, during what is known as the Pannage Season. This is the time when acorns and beech mast lie thick on the ground, a feast for pigs but deadly poisonous to ponies and cattle if eaten in sufficient quantities. One of the Commoners' rights is to turn pigs onto the Forest to pannage. In some areas pigs are allowed to roam throughout the year.

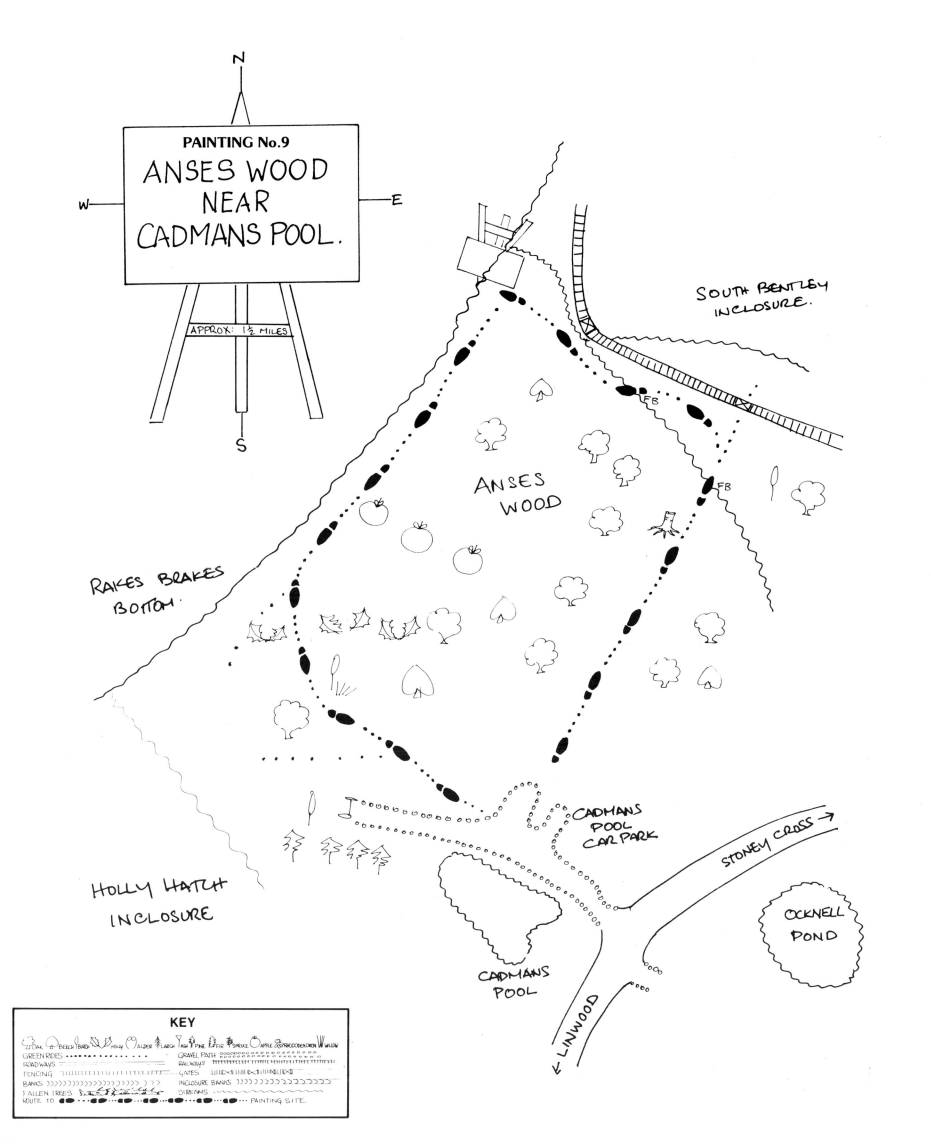

N

W   E

S

PAINTING No.9

ANSES WOOD NEAR CADMANS POOL.

APPROX: 1½ MILES

SOUTH BENTLEY INCLOSURE.

FB

FB

ANSES WOOD

RAKES BRAKES BOTTOM.

CADMANS POOL CAR PARK

STONEY CROSS →

HOLLY HATCH INCLOSURE

CADMANS POOL

OCKNELL POND

← LINWOOD

KEY

OAK   BEECH   BIRCH   HOLLY   ALDER   LARCH   ASH   PINE   FIR   SPRUCE   APPLE   RHODODENDRON   WILLOW

GREEN RIDES ●●●●●●●●●●   GRAVEL PATH ○○○○○○○○○○

ROADWAYS ═══════════   RAILWAYS ▥▥▥▥▥▥▥▥▥

FENCING ┬┬┬┬┬┬┬┬┬┬   GATES ▭▯◁▭▯◁▭

BANKS ≫≫≫≫≫≫≫≫≫   INCLOSURE BANKS ≫≫≫≫≫≫≫≫≫

FALLEN TREES ⌇⌇⌇⌇⌇⌇   STREAMS ∿∿∿∿∿∿∿

ROUTE TO ●●●●●●●●●●●●●● PAINTING SITE.

Highland Water, by Millyford Bridge

Crack. The sound was abrupt. Was it a rifle shot or a whip? Perhaps a branch breaking from a tree. It could have even been someone chopping down a tree. The dogs chasing through the water had prevented our ears from being able to tell. We called our dogs to us and listened. Nothing. Thinking it must have been a branch, we walked on. Crack, crack. We now knew it was not a breaking branch. But, where was it? "I think it's over there!" "No, it's over there." Again we listened and waited. Patience was rewarded. This time the direction was clear so carefully we moved towards it.

The day was bright and warm. Strong summer greens of the oaks fading to ochre. Beech trees glowing with golden patches in amongst the now paler greens. Leaves on silver birches fluttering in the breeze like a mass of tiny yellow and cream butterflies. We paused to admire a clump of foxgloves. Their last few flowers on the tips of long stems still giving sweet nectar to the bees, while fat seed heads were preparing to drop the embryos of future generations.

The sudden resumption of the cracking brought our attention back to the moment. It increased in speed, sounding like kids playing at being swordsmen. Crack, clack, clack, clack, clack. I kept hoping that we would find it to be the one thing we longed to see. A wonderful sound floated through the air. A sound we knew well. The snort of a rutting fallow buck. We looked at each other, excitement mounting. Was that it then, were we really hearing bucks fighting at last?

Realising the wind was blowing the wrong way, we retraced our steps downstream along Highland Water. A bog had to be negotiated and a road crossed before we could find cover where our scent would be carried away from the deer. By the time we reached that position the snorting had been replaced by the crack clacking again. Hazel was, as usual, leading, half crouching as she placed one foot in front of the other. We knew there to be an open area between us and Millyford Bridge beyond. As the trees thinned we crept from behind one to another. And then . . . there they were, only yards in front of us. Two fallow bucks, antlers locked in combat. One pushing so hard his opponent was running backwards. Both grunting furiously. They parted and walked away from one another. Several fallow does were grazing nearby. Some young bucks stood watching from the 'wings'. The two bucks encircled the females, almost meeting at the other end. They turned and walked back towards us. Side by side they came, snorting as they moved, nearly in slow motion. The air was flowing into our faces bringing the tangy musty smell of rutting bucks. With tremendous speed they turned in towards each other, crashing their antlers together in another intense fight. Again and again they hurled themselves into battle. Back feet off the ground and noses in the dirt. My dog was watching this sight in silent amazement. Sally gave a whine. She always likes to join in on a good fight.

My imagination began to run riot believing we were to witness a fight to the death. I winced as the antlers smashed against antlers. I felt sure one would end up blood-stained and broken. To the victor the spoils.

Again they were head to head, earth spraying up from eight hooves desperately trying to stand fast. One buck kept losing ground. He must eventually be the loser I thought. Why doesn't he just give up before he gets hurt? Antlers untangled for a moment. They walked together. Away from us this time. Heads held high and snorting, they moved towards the other younger bucks. This challenge was not taken up. The youngsters took off. One of the big bucks put his head down to graze, the other followed suit. The fighting was over for the moment. After a while we slunk quietly away, no animal having been aware of our presence. We walked back to the car in silence, our minds too full to talk.

Highland Water
BY MILLYFORD BRIDGE

79

Painting No.10

GREY SQUIRREL.

PAINTING No.10

Place: **HIGHLAND WATER, BY MILLYFORD BRIDGE**

Time of Year: November

This is the painting which appears on the cover of the book and the scene is easily viewed from the nearby car park. The water is Highland Water, one of Monica's favourite streams which is lovely throughout its entire length.

Holly trees can be seen in the painting. Holly grows throughout the Forest and is essential for the wildlife as both deer and ponies eat its bark and birds feed on the berries. Small creatures like mice, voles and squirrels will nibble its branches. Deer do not have top teeth (only hard gums) and they eat holly bark by ripping it upwards in long strips. Ponies scissor it off like a human eating an apple.

Ivy grows on the silver birch tree leaning over the stream. This too is an important source of nourishment for animals, particularly roe deer who will eat armfuls of ivy during the bleak winter months.

There are fallen or felled trees lying on the ground throughout the Forest and people may wonder why they are not cleared away. When a person has a licence to collect fallen wood from the Forest, he is required to leave behind about a third to protect the wildlife that lives in dead wood such as insects and fungi. Piles of twigs and branches are left to provide shelter for animals including mice and birds like wrens who will build their nests in such a place.

One of the commonest flowering plants found throughout the Forest, including around Highland Water, is the tormentil. It has tiny yellow flowers and grows close to the ground where animals have cropped the grass short. It first flowers in early spring and carries on right through the summer until autumn.

SIKA AND SALLY

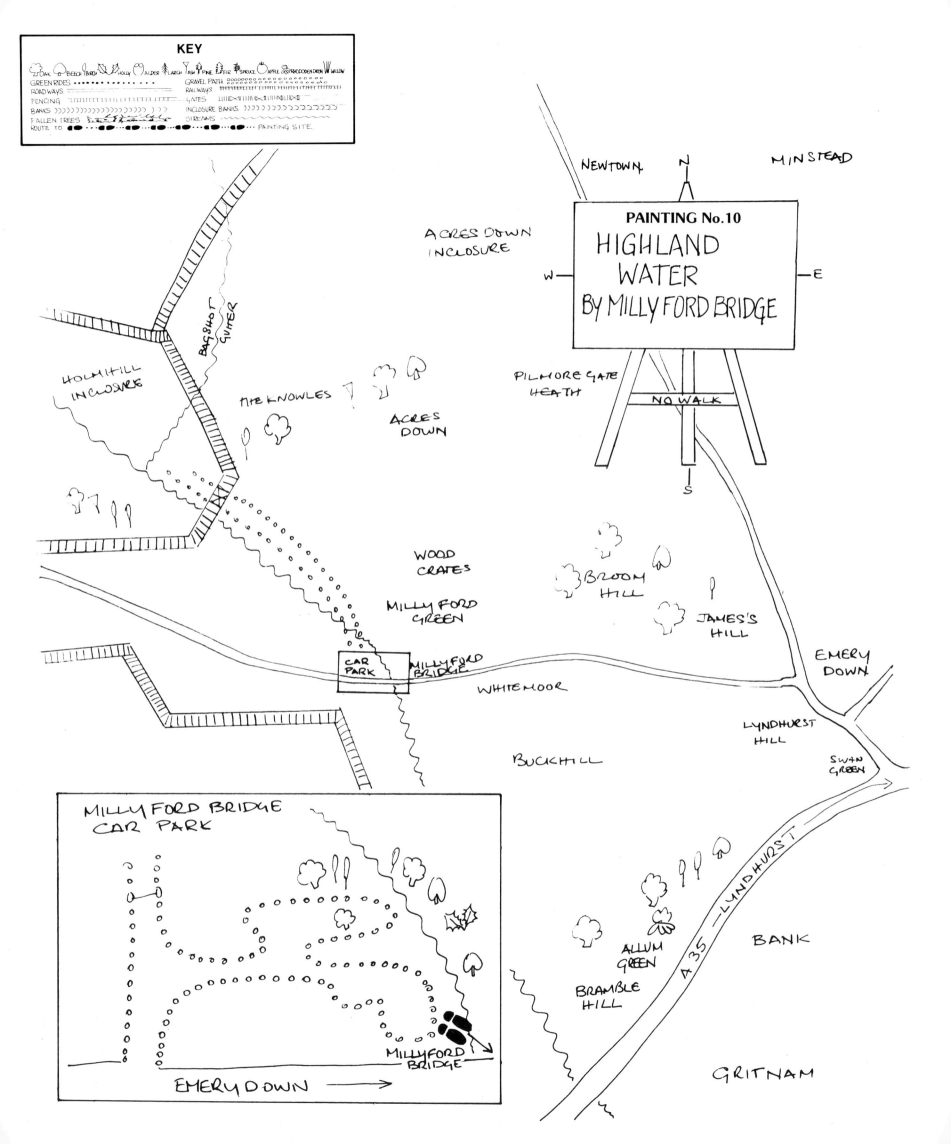

KEY

Oak, Beech, Birch, Holly, Alder, Larch, Ash, Pine, Fir, Spruce, Apple, Rhododendron, Willow

GREEN RIDES ....
ROADWAYS ━━━━━━
FENCING ⊥⊥⊥⊥⊥⊥⊥
BANKS ⟩⟩⟩⟩⟩⟩⟩⟩⟩
FALLEN TREES
ROUTE TO ●●●●●●●●

GRAVEL PATH ○○○○○○○
RAILWAYS ┼┼┼┼┼┼┼
GATES ⊥⊥⊥╳⊥⊥╳⊥⊥
INCLOSURE BANKS ⟩⟩⟩⟩⟩⟩
STREAMS ∿∿∿∿∿∿
PAINTING SITE.

NEWTOWN   N   MINSTEAD

ACRES DOWN
INCLOSURE

PAINTING No.10
HIGHLAND WATER
BY MILLY FORD BRIDGE

W ——— E

NO WALK

S

HOLM HILL
INCLOSURE

BAGSHOT GUTTER

THE KNOWLES

PILMORE GATE HEATH

ACRES
DOWN

WOOD
CRATES

BROOM
HILL

MILLY FORD
GREEN

JAMES'S
HILL

EMERY
DOWN

CAR
PARK

MILLY FORD
BRIDGE

WHITEMOOR

LYNDHURST
HILL

SWAN
GREEN

BUCKHILL

MILLY FORD BRIDGE CAR PARK

ALLUM
GREEN

A 35 — LYNDHURST

BANK

BRAMBLE
HILL

MILLY FORD
BRIDGE

EMERY DOWN ——→

GRITNAM

Winter Sunshine

Brilliant colours of autumn ease slowly down to more subtle shades. Winter gradually takes over. By December the days are short and cold. Sunshine in January can have a wonderful effect, stimulating the mind with memories of summery days to come. The song of a chaffinch can warm spring into the step of cold feet, crunching over frost-hardened snow.

February is often the coldest month. The Forest wildlife have a difficult time finding enough to eat. Squirrels have to dig for hidden nuts. New Forest ponies survive by eating bark. Deer try to conserve energy by moving little.

Although I may see more beauty in winter than many people, the natural world does have several ugly sides to its character. I believe that no animal thinks as we do and in the wild accept their fate without fuss. A starving or old horse will go off alone to die. I've seen a mare and her yearling grazing happily yards from her young foal laying dead in a bog. Birds whose young or eggs have been stolen by a predator build another nest and start again. Insects would probably take over the world were it not for birds. That's nature's way. Living food is eaten by food for something else. And so it goes on, this chain of life. Man is the only weak link, killing out of greed and for fun in the name of sport.

My sport comes from walking in the Forest. My thrills from a lark singing in the middle of March. My fun from searching for cast antlers, and my excitement from catching sight of the first wood violet. I'll stick with nature's way, and go through winter, watching and listening for signs of spring and a new beginning.

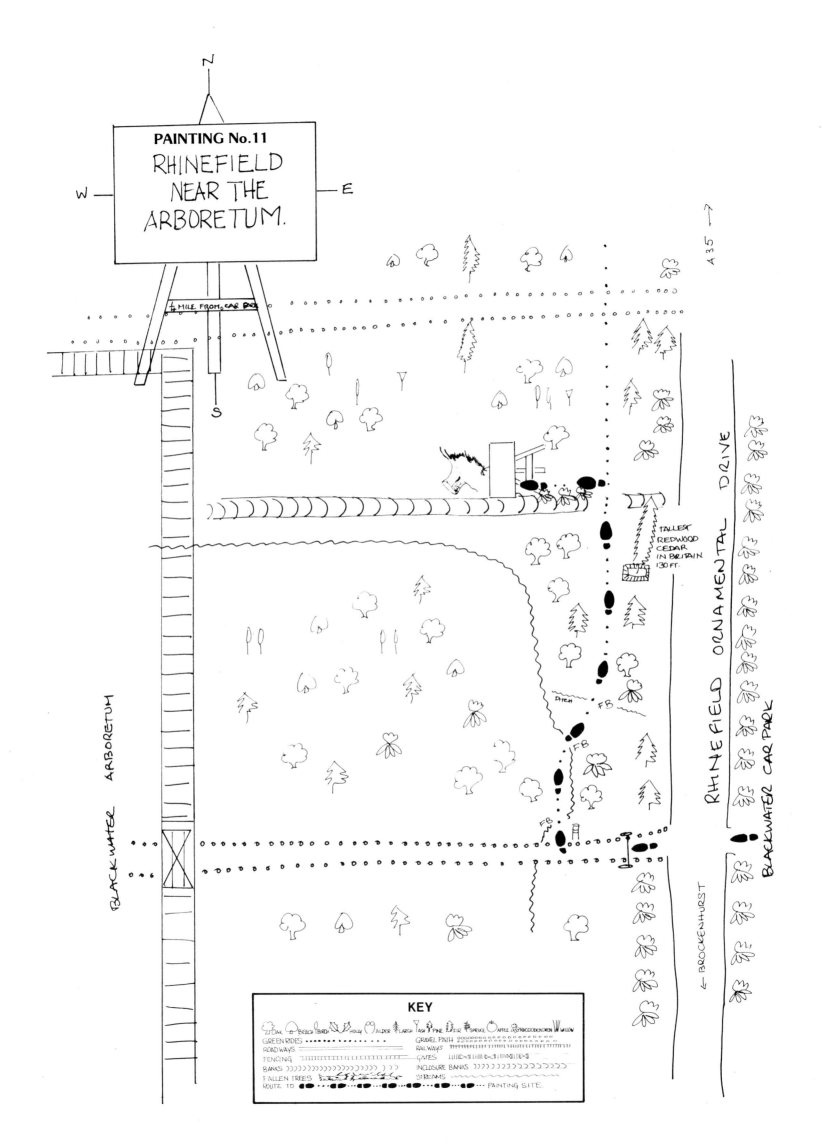

PAINTING No.11

RHINEFIELD
NEAR THE
ARBORETUM.

N
W — E
S

¼ MILE FROM CAR PARK

A 35 →

RHINEFIELD ORNAMENTAL DRIVE

TALLEST
REDWOOD
CEDAR
IN BRITAIN
130 FT.

DITCH
FB
FB
FB

BLACKWATER ARBORETUM

BLACKWATER CAR PARK

← BROCKENHURST

KEY

OAK · BEECH · BIRCH · HOLLY · ALDER · LARCH · ASH · PINE · FIR · SPRUCE · APPLE · CHESTNUT · RHODODENDRON · WILLOW
GREEN RIDES ············
ROADWAYS ————
FENCING
BANKS))))))))))))))))
FALLEN TREES
ROUTE TO ●●●●

GRAVEL PATH ooooooo
RAILWAYS
GATES
INCLOSURE BANKS))))))))))))))
STREAMS ~~~~~~
PAINTING SITE.

PAINTING No.11

Place: **RHINEFIELD, NEAR THE ARBORETUM**

Time of Year: November

Length of Walk: ¼ mile

Memories flood back at this spot for Monica as she remembers it from when her parents brought her. In those days a gate crossed the road where there is now a cattle grid and a Forest urchin would be sitting there waiting to open the gate for a small tip. In later years, Monica in turn brought her parents here so her father could see the spectacular display of rhododendrons, his favourite flower.

The walk from Blackwater car park is both dry and flat and would be suitable for a wheelchair or pushchair. The area is very popular in summer as people come to see the Rhinefield Ornamental Drive and the Tall Trees Walk.

This stand of trees has some of the tallest trees in the country including a Redwood which is at least 137 feet high and has a girth of more than 14 feet. The trees were planted in the middle of the last century along a track which led to the original Rhinefield Lodge, traditionally home of the Keepers of the Forest, and once William the Conqueror's hunting lodge. All 48 trees along the road have been numbered so you can identify them with a Forestry Commission booklet. Among the species are the Black Spruce, Spanish Fir, Indian Deodar, Lawson Cyprus and the strange Wellingtonia which comes from California and lives for over 3,000 years in its native forests.

A new arboretum was planted nearby in 1960 to supplement the mature trees of another ornamental drive at Bolderwood. There are three Forestry Commission walks in the area, all marked out, including the Brock Hill Walk in an area of ancient oaks grown for timber. The walk is named after a small hill topped with beech and oak which has been a badger sett for centuries. 'Broc' was the Old English word for badger.

The stag in this painting is a young red deer in hard antler. During the rut there is never any doubt when red deer are in the vicinity because the stag has a roar like a fog-horn which can be heard for miles around. Unlike sika and fallow, the red stags gather hinds together which they follow around and defend aggressively. Younger stags follow at a safe distance and when the dominant stag becomes exhausted, they take his place in order of age.

During winter, red deer develop a thicker and much darker winter coat. When they begin to moult in spring, like other deer, they can look quite mangey. Great chunks of hair can be found on the ground and if you pick it up and rub it between your fingers it has the same texture as a sable brush.

Rhinefield, near the Arboretum

Mist, dense and white rolling and swirling over the heathland. An early morning sun was trying to break through making an arc like a white rainbow. From out of the crock came not gold but a red deer hind. She stepped gingerly into the road. The driver in front avoided her. I stopped.

With head quite close to the ground she carefully walked across the road. Close behind another followed. More erect this one, younger looking. Then another and several more. As they slowly passed in front of my car, the sun broke through. The light threw the colour up from the heather into the mist creating a gentle pink haze.

Behind this little group of hinds came a red stag. Bigger he seemed than any I had seen before. His neck covered in shaggy hair. With no care for me, my car or the mist, he followed the hinds. As he reached the other side of the road he turned and looked back. I too looked. Four or five young stags were following. He moved towards them. They stopped in their tracks. The big stag turned back to follow the hinds once more. The young opportunists held back, but not for long.

That was some years back now and though I have seen many New Forest red deer since then, I have never seen such a beautiful stag. Recently I was lucky enough to find a cast red deer antler almost completely buried in the undergrowth. Forestry Commission burning off had left the coronet exposed. Antlers of this size are rare so I was lucky to find one so big. It must have lain there for some years and I like to think it may have come from that stag.

Rhinefield
NEAR THE ARBORETUM

87

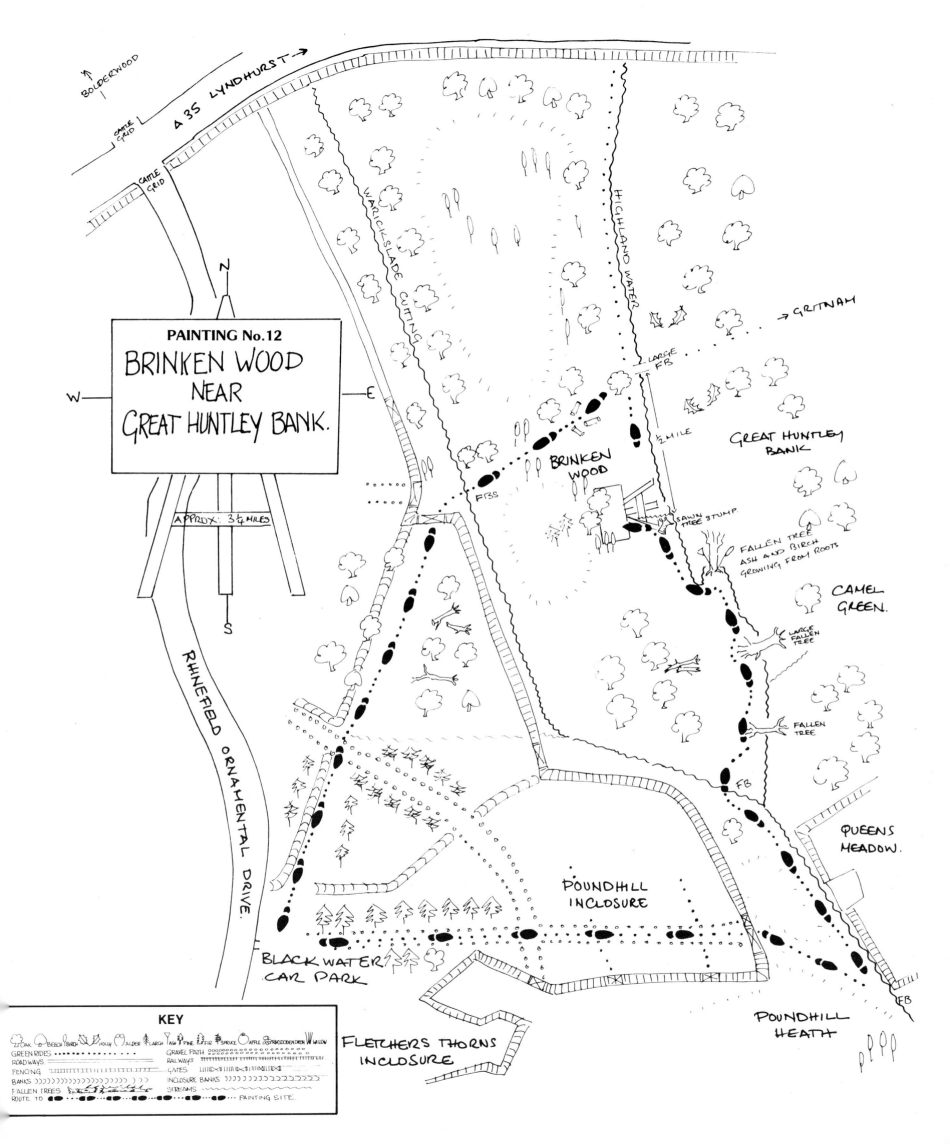

↑ BOLDERWOOD

CATTLE GRID

A 35 LYNDHURST →

CATTLE GRID

N
W — E
S

PAINTING No.12
BRINKEN WOOD
NEAR
GREAT HUNTLEY BANK.

APPROX: 3¼ MILES

WARWICKSLADE CUTTING

HIGHLAND WATER

→ GRITNAM

LARGE FB

½ MILE

GREAT HUNTLEY BANK

BRINKEN WOOD

FBS

SAWN TREE STUMP.

FALLEN TREE
ASH AND BIRCH
GROWING FROM ROOTS

CAMEL GREEN.

LARGE FALLEN TREE

FALLEN TREE

RHINEFIELD ORNAMENTAL DRIVE.

FB

QUEENS MEADOW.

POUNDHILL INCLOSURE

BLACKWATER CAR PARK

FLETCHERS THORNS INCLOSURE

POUNDHILL HEATH

FB

KEY
🌳OAK ⚬BEECH ¥BIRCH ♧HOLLY ⚬ALDER ⁂LARCH ¥YEW ↟PINE ↟FIR ♠SPRUCE ⚬APPLE ⚭RHODODENDRON ※WILLOW
GREEN RIDES · · · · · ·   GRAVEL PATH ∘∘∘∘∘∘∘
ROADWAYS · — · — · —   RAILWAYS +++++++++
FENCING ──────────   GATES ⊞⊞⊞⊞⊞⊞⊞
BANKS)))))))))))))))))   INCLOSURE BANKS)))))))))))))))
FALLEN TREES ⬬⬬⬬⬬⬬⬬   STREAMS ～～～～～
ROUTE TO ●●· · · ●●· · · ●● PAINTING SITE.

Brinken Wood, near Great Huntley Bank

Only twelve hours before we had walked this path, checking its every bump and hole. A straight-forward, easy mile. But now in the pitch black it was a different place. This was 4 a.m. on April 4th, 1985. Escorted by her husband, Alan, Hazel and I were on our way to the 'tower' at Queens Meadow to do a dawn watch.

After driving with car lights it took a moment for our eyes to adjust. Long before half way we were striding along as if in daylight. We arrived at the gate. Have you ever had to go though a five-bar gate silently? It's not as easy as you think. The gravel path crunched like toast and celery under my feet. 'Ssh!'

'I am trying Haze.'

'Sssh!' Haze was creeping along the edge of the path, hardly making a sound. Alan was close behind her. His movement made no sound at all. Haze turned off the path onto a small track towards the tower. We knew the keeper would have unlocked it some time before so Alan was pushed in first. Satisfied that all was safe we sent him off to work. Gently we unbolted and opened the front hatches. This gave us a view across Queens Meadow, only it

was still too dark to see anything. Half an hour or so passed. Two dark shapes became just visible.

'Is that two deer, do you think Haze?'

Yes, it had to be, we could see the shapes moving. Dawn was much slower than we expected. Then quite suddenly the light came in. The meadow was covered in thick pale-green mist. As the mist lifted slightly the two grazing deer transformed themselves into mole hills!

We opened the side hatches and looking out through the west side we could see, very close to us, the upper branches of an oak tree. Like being in a tree house. Memories flooded my mind of the tree house my brother built at 'Riverbend', high in an oak tree in the part of the garden we called 'The Dell'. Crazy paving steps led down to the river where a rowing boat we constantly used was tied up to a jetty. From that tree house you could see for miles up and down the River Stour. I was always a little afraid of climbing up to it. This was a lot easier.

Fast becoming a whiter shade of pale, the mist seemed to move away from us like a carpet being rolled back. Very slowly revealing three fallow does,

then six more. The carpet rolled back a little further. We could hardly believe our luck. There were dozens of them. A feast for the eyes. Seventy-two beautiful fallow does. All ours to watch and marvel at. Nature in all its glory.

Good Friday, April 17th, 1987. I again enjoyed a before-daybreak trip to the same tower. This time my companion was Graham Sirl from the New Forest Deer Protection Council. We arrived just as the sky was lightening the meadow, unseeable from the middle distance onwards. The mist was so white it seemed almost blue. The sun rose ahead and to the right of us. As it did so the mist lifted enough to see many fallow does. We counted thirty-two close by; four bucks, three without antlers and one young pricket.

We heard sounds of a pheasant courting and fighting, a fox, several owls. As dawn came in the bird song increased. Woodpeckers, the green variety, kept calling over towards Great Huntley Bank. The drumming of the Greater Spotted Woodpecker was ringing and echoing through the oak wood along Queens Bower. A kingfisher's piping call caught our attention as it flew down Highland Water just behind the tower.

By the fence at the back of the meadow, beyond which is Hurst Hill Inclosure, we could just make out four white shapes of deer. Suddenly the day broke through as the sun appeared like a golden disc over the trees. The four white deer stood out in a herd of uncountable fallow deer.

A more lovely morning we couldn't have chosen. Wood pigeons cooed in the trees beside us. A heron flew over, its flight path crossing the face of the sun like a Japanese painting. The sun now a little covered by the rising mist changing the colour. Still gold at the top turning pink and lilac and purple at the bottom. A heavy dew on the grass looking almost as a frost.

Yet more does came into the meadow from our right, including a fifth white one. They joined the others and gradually went through the fence into Great Huntley. By 7 a.m. all had left.

On our way back to the car we met two holidaymakers who had found a huge and beautiful fallow buck antler freshly cast. What a prize!

PAINTING No.12

Place:	**BRINKEN WOOD,** **NEAR GREAT HUNTLEY BANK**
Time of Year:	**December/January**
Length of Walk:	**3¼ miles**

Brinken Wood is a very old wood with a lot of silver birch plantations within it. On one side it is flanked by Highland Water and on the other by Warwickslade Cutting. The walk to and from the painting location is flat and easy although it is sometimes muddy at the footbridge after Queens Meadow.

From the footbridge you can cut back over to your right to pick up Highland Water and follow the deer path alongside the stream. Finding the scene of the painting is easy as right by the ditch which is shown in the painting is a cut-down tree and on the face of the stump's surface Monica has carved her initials. The ditch was dug to drain water but fortunately it still lies there making it an ideal subject for a painting.

From the painting you walk on until you come to the old wooden footbridge. Turn south — the path is a little confusing because old sawn-up wood and logs are strewn here and there breaking up the path. Continue as though going straight ahead. As the map shows, you go over two little footbridges. Monica's map does not entirely agree with the Ordnance Survey map and this is one of the few occasions when they have got it wrong! There is a fence with a gate in it which is not marked on the O.S. map. Once through the gate the walk is straight-forward back to the car park.

Fallow deer appear in this picture and the deer platform can be hired from the Forestry Commission. The white fallow deer are not albinos but a rare breed which some say are descendants of a special breed introduced by Charles II. Their young are quite different in colouring from ordinary fallow fawns and are dirty-white or sandy-coloured, becoming creamier as they get older. Fallow young usually have the classic 'Bambi' dappling of white spots, as do red deer young. With fallow the spots are retained in summer whereas red deer lose all their spots at five or six weeks of age.

Two other types of fallow found in the Forest are menil and black fallow but their numbers are small. Menil retain white spots in winter and have a paler coat. Black fallow are one colour — usually a sooty-brown — all over with no white markings. The reason for these different colours is said to be because 'park' deer have been let free into the Forest where they have bred with wild deer and so given the herds interesting variations.

Brinken Wood
NEAR GREAT HUNTLEY BANK

93

YOUNG FALLOW
DOE

Monica and Thelma on a painting trip.

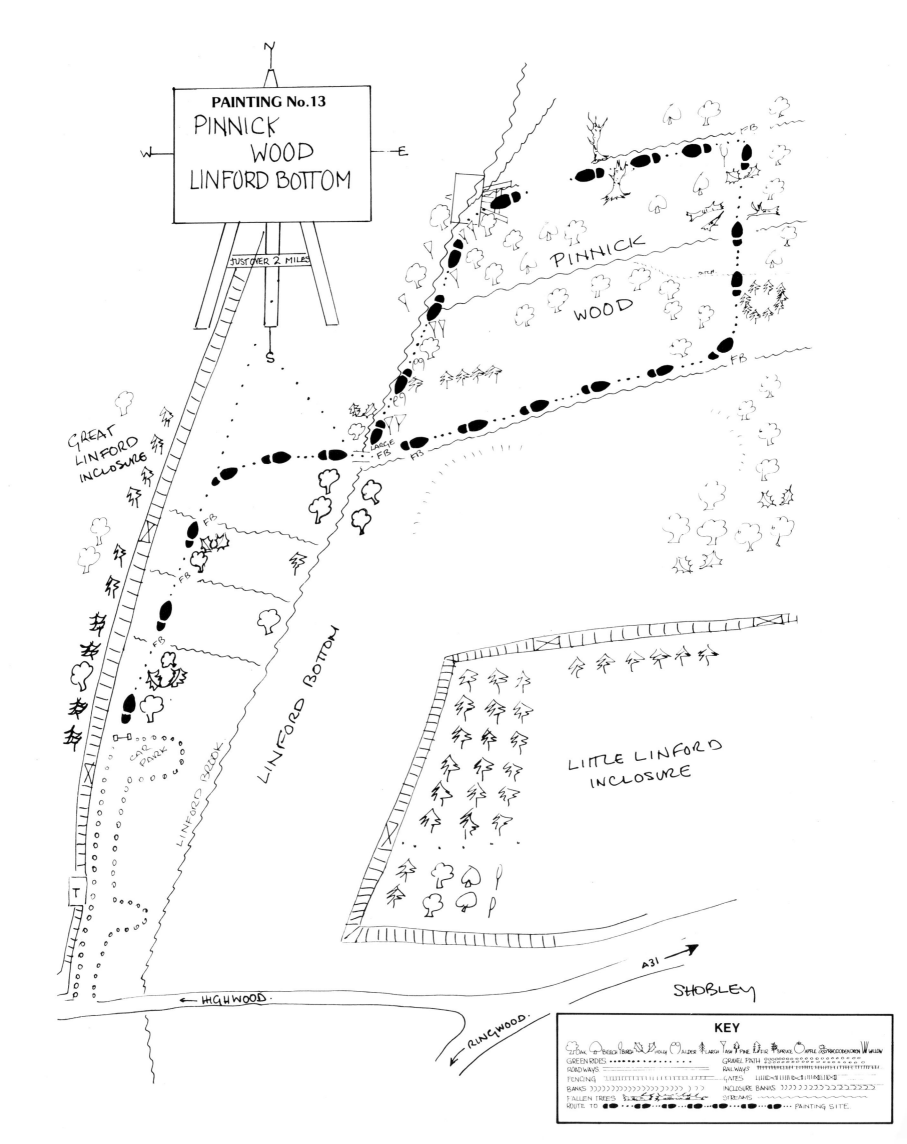

PAINTING No.13

PINNICK WOOD
LINFORD BOTTOM

JUST OVER 2 MILES

PINNICK WOOD

GREAT LINFORD INCLOSURE

FB

FB

LARGE FB

FB

FB

FB

FB

LINFORD BOTTOM

LINFORD BROOK

CAR PARK

T

LITTLE LINFORD INCLOSURE

A31

SHOBLEY

← HIGHWOOD.

↙ RINGWOOD.

KEY

OAK BEECH BIRCH HOLLY ALDER LARCH ASH PINE FIR SPRUCE APPLE RHODODENDRON WILLOW

GREEN RIDES .... GRAVEL PATH oooooooooooo
ROADWAYS ======= RAILWAYS |||||||||||||||||
FENCING TTTTTTTTTTTTTT GATES |||||X|||||X|||||X|
BANKS))))))))))))))) INCLOSURE BANKS))))))))))))))
FALLEN TREES STREAMS
ROUTE TO ●● ●●● ●●● ●● PAINTING SITE.

Place:	**PINNICK WOOD, LINFORD BOTTOM**
Time of Year:	**January**
Length of Walk:	**2 miles**

The walk through this old oak wood where dead and fallen trees lie on the Forest floor, is gentle and flat, both to the painting's location and back. In winter and spring it can be very wet between the car park and the first footbridge.

In spring there are several open patches inside Great Linford Inclosure where bluebells grow but they are smaller than usual because the area is well used by animals and man. This is a favourite place for walking dogs and Monica stresses the importance of keeping a dog under firm control. A dog's natural instinct is to chase something that runs, and many animals, including deer, use the wood. The particular time when dogs should be kept on the lead is in May and June when fawns are being born. In all Inclosures dogs are required to be on a lead.

Pinnick Wood is one of the oldest in the Forest and here the landscape is much as it was in William the Conqueror's time. Then nearly all the forest consisted of deciduous hardwoods, mainly oak and beech. From about the 1770s the look of the Forest began to change as fast-growing softwood conifers were planted. Today, the statutory inclosures contain half coniferous timber and half broad-leaved trees, and the balance is kept to preserve the traditional appearance of the Forest.

The old oak woods are full of interest as they swarm with thousands of tiny living species from beetle larvae which live in the bark to squirrels who collect the nuts. Strange fungi grow on rotten logs and numerous birds live high in the branches. Some of the oldest oaks have lived for 350 years or more.

Within Pinnick Wood are one or two examples of pollarded oak. This was the practice of cutting the top when the tree was young to provide winter food for deer. It was stopped by law in the 18th century when oak was needed for the building of ships as pollarded trees produced inferior timber. Beech trees were also pollarded and some can be seen in the beech woods of Marsh Ash, Ridley and Soarley Beeches. The Forestry Commission has pollarded some young trees alongside the main path through Great Linford inclosure so future generations can see this strange practice. The most famous pollarded tree in the Forest is the Knightwood Oak which is said to be the largest and oldest oak tree in the forest and has a girth of 21 feet.

Wildlife is abundant in Pinnick Wood because it is well away from the main road. In October, sloe berries hang in great blue-black bunches attracting every kind of bird. Ponies, cattle and deer frequent the area including the timid roe deer. In fact, you can see every kind of wildlife found in the Forest in this wood, except the Dartford Warbler.

Roe deer are not encountered frequently as they are solitary animals, occasionally living in small family units. The bucks have small branching antlers and in the summer rut mark out territories where they stay for much of the year. Roe does only come into heat for two days and during that time the buck chases her around and around forming quite distinctive rings in the ground. Although you may not be lucky enough to see a roe, it is quite likely you will come across a roe ring.

Pinnick Wood, Linford Bottom

Quickly I set up the easel. Freezing wasn't the word for it. My hands were feeling stiff already. The scene selected was not in good light. So a brisk walk would help. A sprinkling of snow lay over the ground. Frosted old bracken wet from melting snow, creating a pink haze as steam rose where the sun warmed it, the conductor of an orchestra of colour to excite and delight. Scots Pines looked almost artificial, like Christmas trees sprayed with white frost from a tin.

Sika stood looking back at me, wondering what I had seen. Why had I stopped? What was I gazing at? Behind me Roe Inclosure and Linford Brook. Ahead Great Linford Inclosure. Tall fir trees with oaks behind them. On my right the oaks of Red Shoot Wood showing pale green where moss lay on the bark, mixed with brown tinges. The bracken beneath them dark when hidden from light and pink where sun shone upon it, flecked with white from snow not yet melted. Mauve patches, with pale grey of Scots Pine trunks. My eyes forced to look up as bright rust of younger bark leapt out to demand my attention. Mossy bank covered in virgin snow. Oak trees looming up through the white floor. Reflected light, pale blue, green, pink and white. The fir trees close to me in shadow, very dark. Sudden golden light beyond them as sunshine exploded onto snow-covered bracken. Jays fighting and screaming some distance away. Ivy growing heartily up an oak tree showing the beauty of its bright green leaves to the light.

Fallow deer making tracks in the snow where nothing had been before. With front feet they scrape. Trying to uncover whatever little there may be to eat. Moving slowly so as not to use energy. A lean time for the wild animals now, having to rely on summer fat to survive the winter. Under the oak trees of Red Shoot Wood as it comes down to Greenford Bottom, scratching, fighting and chattering, a mass of Redwings. Little flashes of bright orange from the patches under their wings catching the sun as they flutter and jump about.

The natural world is cruel in many ways yet everything has its place. Birds find food by scratching away the snow in an oak wood uncovering acorns for the deer to eat and so it goes on. Nature is a woven tapestry of colour and texture. Every piece of warp and weft interlocking. Little that exists in the Forest has no use.

Some time later the sunshine disappeared as more snow clouds arrived. A peculiar yellow light covered the scene, growing darker by the second. Eerie and quiet. As I painted fallow bucks walked through by the stream beyond. Two more came from behind. One much younger than the other. Sika watched with one front paw raised, natural instincts to chase stirring within her. Knowing she must not, just watched. Snow began to fall. The human, who had the choice, packed up and went home to the central heating.

Pinnick Wood
LINFORD BOTTOM

Painting No.13

ROE BUCK.

Shepton Water
NEAR BEAULIEU

Painting No.14

SIKA STAG

Shepton Water, near Beaulieu

Softly we crept along the path, dogless today. A species of deer that live between Brockenhurst and Beaulieu is the Japanese Sika and this day we were out to see them. We obeyed the signs telling us to keep to the gravel paths. We had only ever seen a small group of hinds once before. Even then it was only the noise that made us realise they were not fallow. Hinds, as well as stags, make a high pitched alarm call. Frighten the life out of you it will the first time you hear it!

Ahead we could see a grass ride crossing the path. As we reached it, there feeding on our left were two sika stags. One, his back a rich golden brown with a black stripe running along the spine; his neck varying shades of grey, antlers dark brown, tinged and tipped with cream. With his back to us I could see his white rump, quite different from that of fallow. The black edging to the white doesn't stand out, the sika stag being a darker-coated animal. The fallow have nine inch tails — the sika only six inches. In fallow, the shape of the white area is elongated, running down the inside of the back legs. The sika rump is more heart-shaped and they have lighter legs than fallow. The second stag was almost black. Both had good antlers. Eight points.

We had read that stags were very secretive and rarely seen, so we felt privileged to crouch behind a moss-covered bank and watch these lovely creatures grazing. The sunlight flickered through constantly moving leaves of an oak tree onto the two stags showing a steel blue-grey on the black one's neck. As if he had become aware of our presence, the dark sika raised his head and looked straight at us. We didn't move. We dared not. For some two or three minutes he stared. A pale U-shaped marking gave his

face a ghostly mask-like look. He turned and quietly disappeared into the undergrowth. The brown stag soon followed.

I looked at Haze. Binoculars still to her eyes, she was gently smiling. If only those animals could have known what pleasure they had given to two daft humans.

We have returned to that area many times since. Several sika stags have stood and stared. We've watched stags fighting. We've even been brave enough to hire the tower near Brockenhurst to watch the rut. But no sight could compare with our first look at those two stags. When I say sight, I mean sight. For a sound did compare. We'd read a book written by a lady who had studied sika deer and were anxious to hear the stag's call which she had found so difficult to describe.

One autumn day we arrived at the chosen spot. Along a path beside an oak wood, we found cover and settled down to wait. We had no idea what to expect. Would we know the sound if we heard it? In silence we waited, and waited. Beginning to yawn now. Enthusiasm draining away. Fidgeting, stretching, drawing pictures in the earth with a lethargic finger. I don't know whether Haze was yawning and got stuck, or if her jaw just dropped! I know mine did. We looked at each other, eyes and mouths wide open. Ears not believing the sound that had penetrated them. We know now why that lady found no adequate words to describe the mating call of the sika stag. A high-pitched whistle like scream winding down to a groan. That's the best I can do. Go, hear it for yourself, you will not be disappointed.

PAINTING No.14

Place: SHEPTON WATER, NEAR BEAULIEU
Time of Year: March

This painting finishes the seasonal cycle and brings us back to spring. The walk is very short, only about 300 yards along the stream from the road.

One of the observation towers which can be rented from the Forestry Commission is in Frame Inclosure near Brockenhurst. (Another is in Queens Meadow — see Painting No. 12). In Frame the tower is deep within a thick wood which is very dark at night. You have to cross a stream and climb a perpendicular ladder to enter through a hatch in the floor — an excursion not for the faint-hearted!

Watching sika deer from thick foliage is like being in a fairy grotto where you can see nothing around you except light dancing through the dense pall of leaves and the only sound is the whistling of stags to the hinds. When pale light falls on them they seem uncanny as the striped facial markings give them glowering expressions just like human skulls.

Sika are smaller than fallow and sometimes walk with a graceful slow-motion gait called 'stilting' when they lift their feet high like dressage ponies.

SIKA STAG

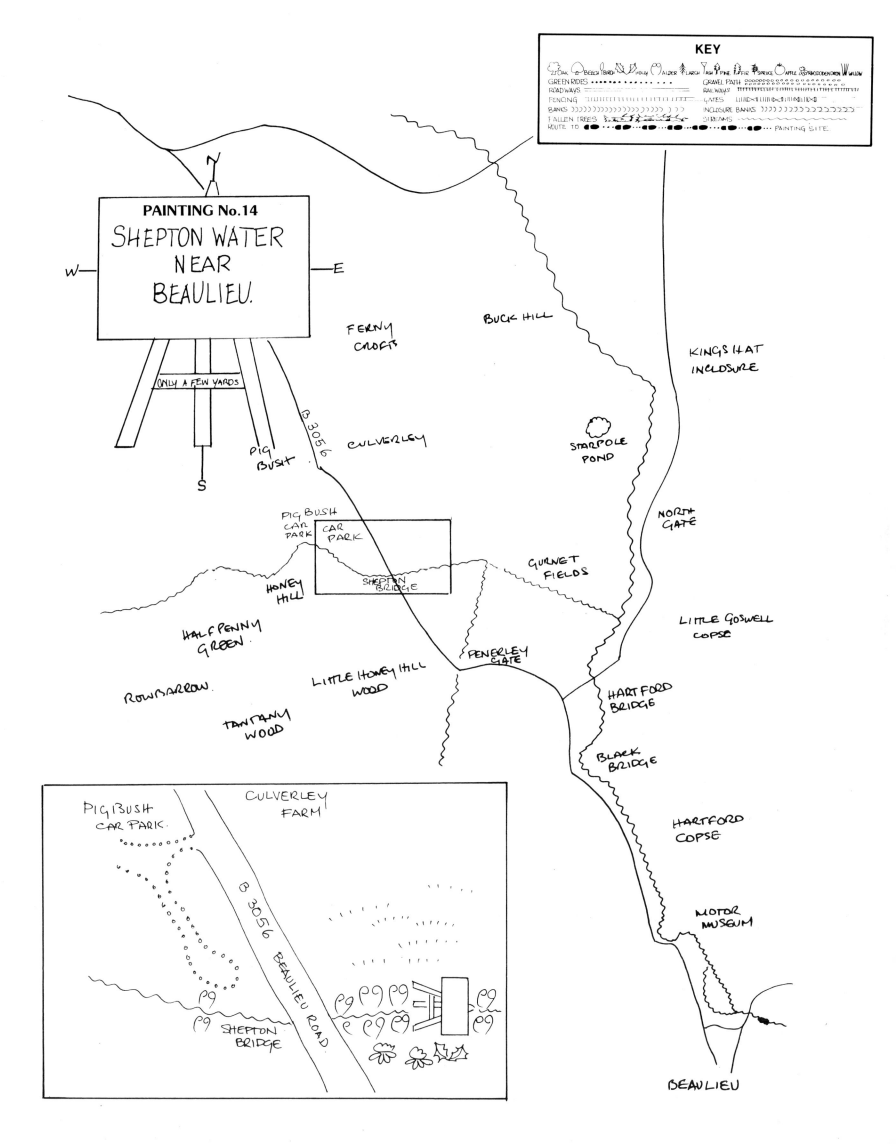

KEY

OAK BEECH BIRCH HOLLY ALDER LARCH ASH PINE FIR SPRUCE APPLE RHODODENDRON WILLOW

GREEN RIDES ········
GRAVEL PATH ∘∘∘∘∘∘∘∘∘∘
ROADWAYS ═══════
RAILWAYS ┼┼┼┼┼┼┼┼┼┼┼
FENCING ⊥⊥⊥⊥⊥⊥⊥⊥⊥⊥⊥
GATES ▭⊣⊢▭
BANKS)))))))))))))))))
INCLOSURE BANKS))))))))))))))
FALLEN TREES ⋙⋙⋙⋙
STREAMS ∿∿∿∿∿∿
ROUTE TO ●●●●●●●●●●●● PAINTING SITE

PAINTING No.14

SHEPTON WATER NEAR BEAULIEU.

W —— E

S

ONLY A FEW YARDS

FERNY CROFTS

BUCK HILL

KINGS HAT INCLOSURE

PIG BUSH

B 3056

CULVERLEY

STARPOLE POND

NORTH GATE

PIG BUSH CAR PARK

CAR PARK

SHEPTON BRIDGE

GURNET FIELDS

HONEY HILL

LITTLE GOSWELL COPSE

HALF PENNY GREEN

PENERLEY GATE

ROWBARROW

LITTLE HONEY HILL WOOD

HARTFORD BRIDGE

TANTANY WOOD

BLACK BRIDGE

HARTFORD COPSE

MOTOR MUSEUM

PIG BUSH CAR PARK.

CULVERLEY FARM

B 3056 BEAULIEU ROAD

SHEPTON BRIDGE

BEAULIEU

PART III

Walking in the Forest

For anyone thinking of taking up walking, the New Forest is ideal. Most of it is fairly flat but with just enough hills to make you puff a bit!

Footwear is, of course, very important. You need a pair of waterproof boots — I prefer the type with soft tops, back and sides but strong soles. I usually wear two pairs of socks, all cotton next to my feet with thicker ones on top. Every time I stop to rest on a long walk in hot weather I take off my boots and socks — if only for a few minutes. It's wonderfully refreshing.

Clothes too are important, particularly in winter. I wear cord trousers tucked into long socks like an American soldier and a hooded, thermal-lined coat that comes down to my knees. I have varying degrees of thermal underwear, a thermal jumper and a number of sleeveless body warmers in different thicknesses. Everything is green to blend with the background — essential for watching animals. Certainly not a glamorous outfit but I have never felt cold even in the most biting wind.

On day walks one of us carries a haversack for food and drink and a small first aid kit for emergencies. I have a piece of strong string in my pocket and a multi-bladed penknife which has a saw (useful if you have to cut a splint), a pair of scissors and a prong for removing stones from horses' hooves. I haven't had to use the latter yet even though my 'donkey' gets stones in her boots sometimes!

If you want to watch animals, then a pair of binoculars is essential. I always carry a stick as it works wonders when crossing streams and ditches, is good to lean on when watching wildlife and is useful for pulling down that bit of honeysuckle for a closer look.

Most important of all, always carry a map and a compass. Once inside a plantation it is very easy to lose your sense of direction and you can wander around aimlessly for hours. It can be quite a frightening experience. The best map I have found is:

The Ordnance Survey Outdoor
Leisure Map of the New Forest
1 : 25,000 (No. 22)

The Forestry Commission has numerous walks and trails in the Forest. Their observation towers for watching deer can only be used by prior arrangement. Details can be obtained from:

The Forestry Commission,
Queens House,
Lyndhurst,
Hants. SO43 7NH

There is so much beauty to be seen in the Forest it is impossible to ever be bored. When watching animal wildlife it is important to assess the air flow. It must be in your face so your scent is blown away from the animal's sensitive nose. Most animals cannot see as far as humans and if you keep still within the landscape they won't know your shape from that of a bush or tree. Even if you are close enough to be seen, try to make sure there is a tree, a bush or even a hill behind you and, so long as green or dark clothing is worn, you will blend into the background.

Wild creatures do not just rely on their sense of smell but also on their hearing which is acute. I have spent ages creeping on hands and knees to get a closer look, only at the last second to crack a twig and in an instant it's gone. With birds, movement is the thing which worries them most, so it is best to keep still as much as you can.

The Forest is there for all of us to enjoy, so go out and discover your own New Forest. Whether you walk or paint, there is plenty to see and do. But remember that nature or wildlife study can't be done in a hurry. You need time to spare, time to waste, time to learn about your subject. Time just to sit and listen, to observe with love and care. Time to concentrate and great, great patience.

DARTFORD WARBLER
TAIL WAGS IN FLIGHT

Hazel Jackson joins Monica for a walk in the Forest.

Painting Techniques and Tips

This chapter is meant for the beginner or amateur artist who wishes to try painting with knives. The 'experts' will tell you that to be able to paint, one must be able to draw. I don't go along with that theory. I believe anyone can paint. For several years now I have been privileged to judge children's painting competitions and the effects that can be achieved with imagination and colour are wonderful. So if you can't draw, don't be put off, have a go.

Come with me now on a painting trip into the New Forest and I'll do my best to show you how I go about painting. I can't tell you how you should paint, you must experiment for yourself. All I can do is tell you my way. Find your own way and practice as much as you can.

Equipment

Start with the six colours I use — illustrated in the drawing. Add later if you need different colours to suit your style of work. You will need a palette on which to mix your paint. I use a piece of plate glass the correct shape to fit into my box easel. For those who paint outdoors a lot, a box easel is very useful. It folds into a carryable size. The three knives I suggest should be enough to get you started. When I began painting, a canvas was not affordable. So I cut hardboard and covered it with household paint undercoat or sometimes even emulsion. But I found my work improved dramatically when I first used a canvas. Get someone to give you one for Christmas.

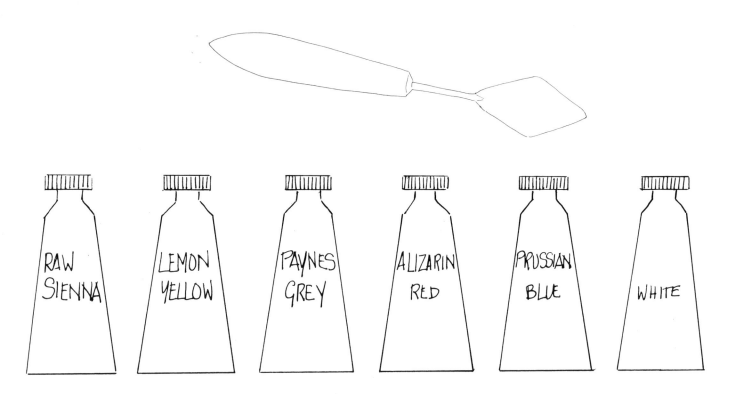

RAW SIENNA   LEMON YELLOW   PAYNES GREY   ALIZARIN RED   PRUSSIAN BLUE   WHITE

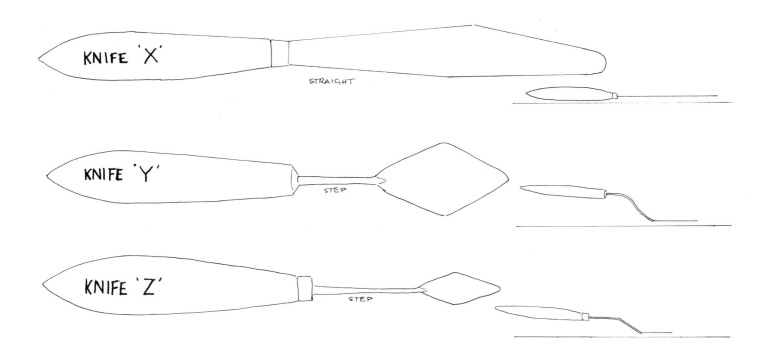

Often I am asked by would-be painters how to start. The first thing is to arrange your own mind. When you buy canvas and paint for the first time imagine you would be prepared to throw it all away. That way you will not worry so much about not producing a good picture. Just have a go and practice. Don't forget you can always scrape the paint off the canvas, clean with turps and re-use. I always carry a small jar of turps in my easel for cleaning palette and knives. My other essential item of equipment is a toilet roll which has a hundred and one uses when painting in the Forest!

Although it is difficult to explain any action with words (and, of course, everyone's interpretation is different), if you've already tried painting, chances are it's been with brushes. To use knives is not at all the same. If you have ever iced a cake you are nearer to the ways of painting with knives than those who are competent with brushes. Think of the canvas as a piece of bread and the paint as butter. Try not to mix the colours too much. Back to the kitchen again for a moment — you fold colours together like putting the sugar into egg-whites when making meringues. More excitement can be created by folding than mixing. The slightest introduction of one colour to another will produce a variety of hues and tones.

To make a scene into a picture the artist sometimes needs to use 'artist's licence'. Composition is important. God may have made that tree too straight, so bend it a little. Add one or leave one out.

Ready to Go!

There are a number of different actions using
the three knives, and I have illustrated them below:

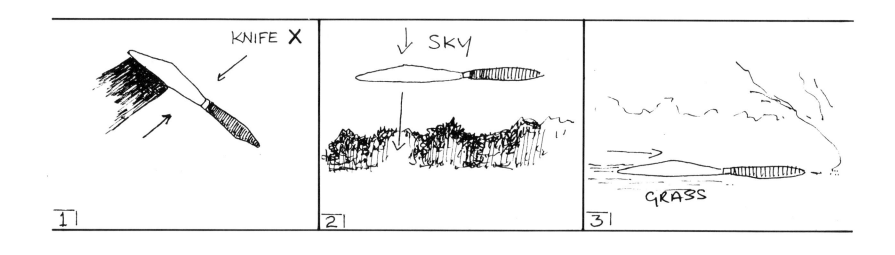

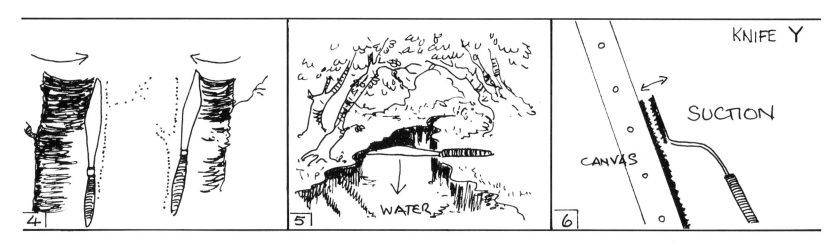

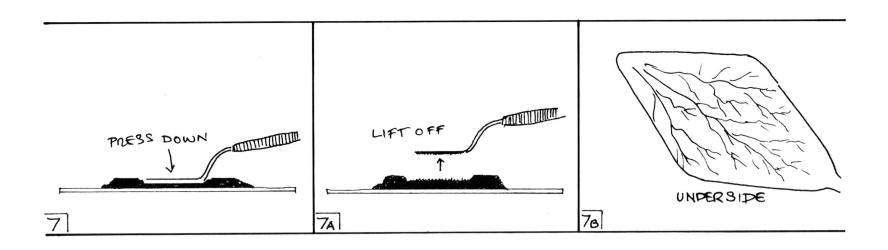

7 PRESS DOWN

7A LIFT OFF

7B UNDERSIDE

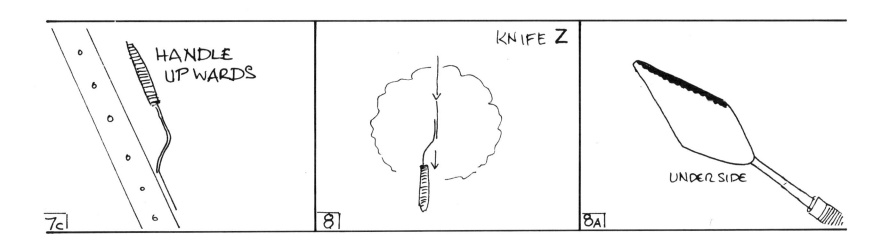

7C HANDLE UPWARDS

8 KNIFE Z

8A UNDERSIDE

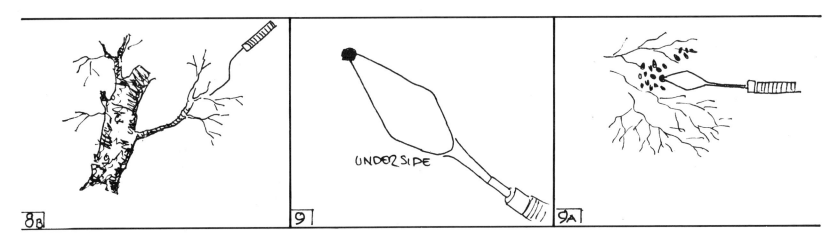

8B

9 UNDERSIDE

9A

I have chosen a simple forest scene and I will take you through painting it step by step. Each step is marked with a letter.

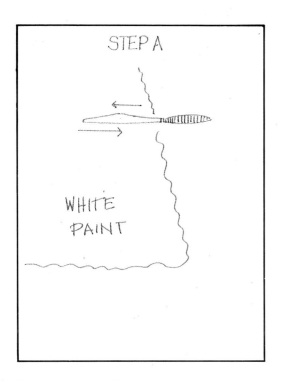

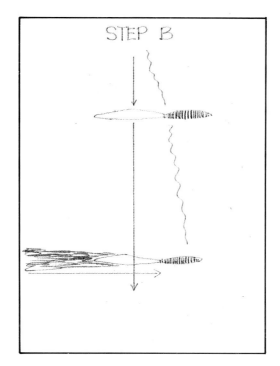

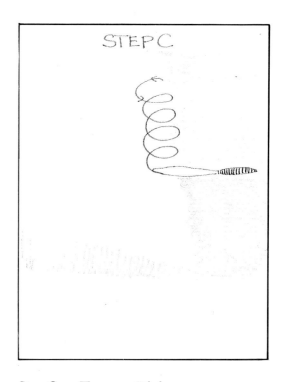

Step A — The Sky

Using White and Knife 'X' apply thinly over canvas as in Drawing 1 and 2 — just like spreading butter, but be mean with it! Mix a little Prussian Blue with White and add to the White on the canvas with short to-and-for action.

I keep skies simple. Too much sky detail can, in my opinion, detract from a painting. You need to experiment. Don't fight too hard to copy the sky you can see. Try to create a background for your painting. Always blend sky colours on the canvas. Once colours are mixed on the palette they become one dense colour; blending on the canvas I find gets a better effect.

Step B — Background Trees

Still with Knife 'X' cover the canvas in the area of background trees using a folded mixture of Paynes Grey and Lemon Grey with a tiny spot of Prussian Blue. Apply using a firm long movement across the canvas.

Now add a little White, a little Paynes Grey and a little Raw Sienna and put it in rough streaks (not mixed) over the top of the green. With the flat of the knife blend together in small circular movements.

Wipe from the knife every trace of paint. Place flat of the blade firmly onto the paint of your sky at the top of your canvas and draw the knife down over the top edges of background trees and down past their base (Drawing 2). If you can master this action it will give a soft edge to the trees which will help to create the illusion of distance. Wipe the knife clean each time or your sky will end up the same colour.

At the base of the background trees, to give an impression of distance, use Knife 'X' in a circular action to give textural shape to trees a little nearer.

Step C — Trees on Right

Cover the canvas with a dark mixture of Raw Sienna and Paynes Grey (50 : 50) using Knife 'X' in the same way as sky was applied. Blend edge of trees to sky with circular motion.

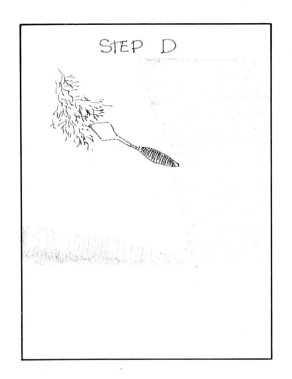

Step D — Tree on Left

Change to Knife 'Y'. Fold together a little Lemon Yellow, less Paynes Grey, a tiny spot of Prussian Blue and a little White. Spread the mixture about an eighth-of-an-inch thick on the palette. Press the flat bottom side of the blade of Knife 'Y' down onto the paint (Drawing 7), then lift off (Drawing 7a). Look at the underside of your knife. You will see that a pattern has been made (Drawing 7b). Very gently and carefully place that pattern over dark areas (Drawing 7c) almost without allowing the knife to touch the canvas.

When applying foliage the handle of the knife should be pointing in the same direction the foliage is growing.

Step E — Foliage of Trees on Right

Apply as in Drawings 7, 7a, 7b and 7c using a mixture of Lemon Yellow and Paynes Grey, to make a rich green.

Step F — Trunks

Back to Knife 'X'. Fold a mixture of Raw Sienna with Paynes Grey making a dark mixture. Spread a little paint on the palette and then draw knife edge through the paint so there is a thin line of paint on the edge, the same as in Drawing 8a. (Knife 'Z' can be used for trunks if you prefer.) Apply edge of knife to canvas as in Drawing 4, moving from left to right.

Now mix a little White into the dark mixture on palette and apply as in Drawing 4 moving from right to left.

Tree trunks and branches need a great deal of study. You must experiment. Bark is not just brown or just green. Look carefully and you will see many different colours. The colours I have suggested are basic colours.

Step G — Branches

Branches are applied using Knife 'Z' and a folded mixture of Paynes Grey and Raw Sienna, in the manner of Drawings 8, 8a and 8b.

The first time you put the knife on the canvas, the paint is thick, so build the branches from trunk outwards, as the paint gets thinner with each application — just as branches get thinner at their extremities.

Step H — Grass

Apply a line of folded Lemon Yellow, Paynes Grey and White under the base of background trees using Knife 'X'. Then pull knife to the right as in Drawing 3.

Fold Lemon Yellow and Paynes Grey using a little more Grey than before, and cover canvas where grass should be.

Now take Knife 'Y' and fold Lemon Yellow, Paynes Grey with perhaps a little Raw Sienna and apply paint to canvas with stipple-suction movement as in Drawing 6. White and Lemon Yellow will add highlights.

Remember you can put light over dark and dark over light but not light onto light. For bracken areas use folded mixture of Raw Sienna with a tiny spot of Alizarin Red and White.

Step I — Water

A dark mixture is used for water because light goes over the top of it easier. Use a 50 : 50 mixture of Paynes Grey and Raw Sienna. Using Knife 'X' apply the colour in 'blobs' under the edge of the bank. Then, pressing the knife into the paint, pull downwards as in Drawing 5. This gives the effect of depth and shadows in the water.

To put lighter areas of reflected sky into the water, apply sky colour in 'blob' and draw the knife down again. This can also be done for reflections of foliage using a green mixture. Continue building up the water in this way.

Using Knife 'Z' as in Drawing 9 and Drawing 9a, leaves floating on water can be achieved.

The surface of water can be suggested by Knife 'Z' with the action of Drawing 8, 8a and 8b.

A few horizontal white lines laid in random across the water will give it an appearance of movement. Apply with Knife 'Z' as in Drawings 8 and 8a.

Step J — Grassy Bank

Apply as for grass, Step H.

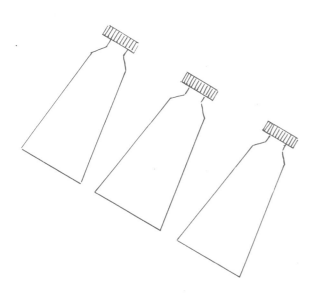

Step K — Stones on edge of Water

Using a darkish mixture of Paynes Grey and Raw Sienna, apply small spots of paint as in Drawings 9 and 9a, using Knife 'Z'.

Over the top of this put Raw Sienna mixed with White, again in small spots as Drawings 9 and 9a. In some cases the lighter spots will completely cover the darker ones thus giving the impression of light and shade.

Don't despair if all does not go as well as you had hoped. Remember you can always scrape the paint off a canvas and begin again!

Tips on Colours

All the colours I have mentioned are basic and you should experiment and find the mixtures you feel suit the subject best. The following is a rough guide of colours for leaves:

Colours of Leaves — Brown

Oak:

Raw Sienna — add small mixture of Lemon Yellow and Paynes Grey. Warm with Alizarin Red.

Silver Birch:

Lemon Yellow — add small amount of Raw Sienna mixed with spot of Alizarin Red.

Beech:

Mix Raw Sienna with small amount of Alizarin Red. Fold together a mixture of Lemon Yellow and Raw Sienna and a mixture of Lemon Yellow and Alizarin Red.

Add white to lighten and highlight or Paynes Grey to make in shadow.

Colours of Leaves — Green

Fir:

> *Raw Sienna — add tiny amount of Prussian Blue. To highlight add Lemon Yellow.*

Oak:

> *Raw Sienna — add Lemon Yellow for early spring.*
> *For summer Lemon Yellow mixed with touches of Paynes Grey and Raw Sienna.*

Silver Birch:

> *For spring — Lemon Yellow. Add very small mixture Raw Sienna with a spot of Prussian Blue.*
> *Add White.*
> *For summer — Lemon Yellow, Paynes Grey. To highlight add White.*

Beech:

> *Spring — Lemon Yellow and small amount of Paynes Grey and White.*
> *Summer — Lemon Yellow and Paynes Grey.*

To create the feeling of distance add White with a tiny spot of Prussian Blue.

Ivy:

> *Lemon Yellow and Paynes Grey. Add White to Lighten, Prussian Blue for shadow.*

Where to Paint?

Choosing the right spot to set up your easel may, at first, be difficult. Begin by deciding what kind of scene pleases your eye most. If it is open countryside, then the New Forest has plenty of heathlands with views — Godshill, Fritham Plain, Berry Wood looking across Harvest Slade. Boltons Bench and along the Beaulieu Road. If it is trees and water, try Millyford Bridge car park or Puttles Bridge or Holidays Hill and the Roman arch.

The face of the New Forest is beautiful almost all over. But it does have a few blemishes, mostly man-made. Environmentalists find ugliness in plantations of fir trees and I understand that feeling very well. From an artist's viewpoint they have little to offer on their own, but the Forest does have to earn a living and there is great commercial demand for the timber.

Although I try to paint as far afield as I can, I do have my favourite areas. South Oakley is lovely to paint and very easy to get at. All around Burley and Rhinefield beauty abounds right beside the road and into the depths. Brockenhurst, Fritham, Lyndhurst, have wonders of their own. I have painted Dockens Water from Queens North Wood through splash bridge to Moyles Court. Highland Water from Woolsmoor Meads to Ivy Wood, by then the Lymington River as it disappears out to sea through private land. I have painted at Beaulieu and along Shepton Water.

Go and find the type of New Forest scenery you like best. I hope you'll have as much pleasure as I do from creating a painting. It is a satisfying hobby at any age — and remember I didn't really begin until I was in my forties! Find your own way and practice as much as you can. Above all have a go and have fun. I'm sure you'll never regret the experience.

Everyone needs something to look forward to while hanging on to the past. Working on this book has fulfilled all those needs in me. Talking endlessly to Anne Ruffell, I have looked back through paper thin shadows to the early years of my life and with her enthusiasm, skill and guidance I have stepped forward into a new world of words. I will always be grateful to her.

My thanks must also be expressed to some other important people.

MARIE ANDREWS
Who opened new doors in my mind

ERIC AND EILEEN ASHBY
They shared with us the secret world of Vicky and Sheba

PAUL CAVE
His faith in my work gave me confidence

THELMA GOULD
She has listened patiently while the would-be writer read aloud, page after page, after page

HAZEL JACKSON
Together, we always have "the best of the day"

JUNE MYERS
A very special thanks

LEN NICHOLLS
It was his idea to have a techniques section

PAUL PENROSE FINE PHOTOGRAPHY
For his care and attention to colour

GRAHAM SIRL
Because he is the backbone of the cause I hold most dear

FORESTRY COMMISSION KEEPER DEREK THOMPSON
He allowed Anne and me the privilege of being so close to Fallow deer.

AND TO MY CUSTOMERS, MY FAMILY AND MY FRIENDS

Colin Andrews
Margaret Andrews
Eric & Eileen Ashby
Phoebe Daisy Aspry
Bernard & Celia Ashley
Lynne Patricia Atkinson
Jan Attrill
Marie Andrews
Peter & Litte Andrews
John & Eileen Attenborough
Catherine Ann Adams
Jill M. Alderson
Mrs. T. Atchley
Charles Budden
Alistair Neil Bain
Penelope V. Barker
Dorothy Francis Barton
Mr. & Mrs. J. M. Barter
Margaret J. K. Betteridge
Ronald N. Beale

Stuart Michael Burton
David & Annie Benfield
Alan & Rosemary Boswell —
Camping International
Walter & Margaret Burrows
Ronald Peter Blewett
John & Christine Bassage
Gillian & William Bennett
John Lees Baxter
Leslie Brown
Sue & Steve Brinkman
Olive Brett
Cynthia Mary Broomfield
F. M. Belsham
J. M. Bogh
R. C. Bryant
Amanda Burke
Sarah Broadhurst
Derek & Janet Burt
Lionel Frederick Batholomew

Christopher & Phyllis Barnes
Clive John Badger
Mr. & Mrs. K. B. Brookes
Kathleen Buckman
George & June Bentham
Alan & Irene Brown
Alison Jean Bodley
Gillian Burrows
Jean Bright
Tony Brewer
John Barradell
Joan & Bob Baylis
Hazel K. Barnes
Barton Cat Sanctuary
Kenneth Francis Blake
Holly Bassage
Dawn Vivien Breese
Carol Bartlett
Judy & Brian Boulanger —
Oakfield Lodge

Iris Clarke
Norman Chislett
J. E. Corker
Daniel Crombie Clifton
Andrew Cameron
Mr. & Mrs. J. D. Coppack
Mrs. A. N. Coppack
Doreen Peggy Clark
Janet, Sophie & Michael
Coleman-New
Anthony John Cuss
Robert Cross
Margaret Croft
Richard & Christine Clarke
Unita Joy Chamberlain
Mr. & Mrs. M. Clampin
Shirley Cano-Lopez
Brian William Currie
David John Cox
Gill Coveney

Brian M. Cox
Joy & Maurice Cousins
Clare & John Chubb
Joan Carpenter
Iris B. Cowley
Robert G. Churchill
Rod & Ruth Collins
Debbie & Francis Carmody
Christopher & Sharne Compton
Audrey Lilian Collins
John Harry Coleman
George & Diana Collins
Charles Cleaver
Colin Creasey
Leslie Crowther
Edeltraut Hildegard Cobb
Philip & Rebecca Coakley
Valerie Crabb
Christopher Cutler
Robert John Cottingham
Jackie & Keith Coello
Morfydd C. Deri-Bowen
Ann Deri-Bowen
Terry Dean
William John Dean
Michael & Caroline Donachie
Vera Donachie
Lyndy & Ken Dean
Eric James Dunkason
Edward R. Davis
Tim & Lindsay Drew
Valerie Duffin — *Parkside Galleries*
Muriel Doris Diamond
Grahame E. G. Dean
Margaret Helen Dollery
Mrs. Judy Dent
Madge Donald
Ethelberta Dalziel M.B.E.T.D.
Mrs. V. F. Day
Kitty D'Arcy
Dawn D'Arcy
Irene Edith Duff
Joan D'Avoine
F. J. Dashley
Mrs. A. Elliott
Mr. M. A. Edgington
Wendy Edwards
Eileen Englefield
Lilian Emery
Roy Desmond Ernest Fielder
Gp. Capt. & Mrs. W. E. French
Olive Freeman
Pamela Irene Field
William Foggon
Valerie Desme Flowers
Mr. & Mrs. A. Fox
Rose & Samuel Fulham
Lily May Finch
Sheila Frances
Barbara Fensham
Hilary Finn
Roy Forrest
Mr. & Mrs. Friend
John A. Flack
Tessa F. M. Fowler
Colin & Gill Flexon
Jennifer Ferrone
Clive & Sue Fisher
Framecraft Ringwood
Jean Gasson
Patricia E. Guy
Tom & Audrey Green

Florence S. Galton
Susan Gould S.R.N.
Jean Griffiths
Joan W. Gray
Rosemary Gray
Reginald Brian Gee
Derek Gibbs
Janet Elaine Gill
John Francis Gibbs
Monica Gibbons
Sheila Gray-Geary
Edwin Goodyear —
Waggon & Horses
Sheila Francis Galloway
Thelma Shirley Gould
Ethel Vera Hendy
Poppy Hooper
Barbara Mary Hadler
Gillian Mary Ellen Habbin
David & Betty Hayter — *Clockmaker*
George & Mary Hay
Doreen & Gerry Hooper
Patrica & Patrick Higgins
Gladys M. Haines
Ronald & Elsa Haynes
Leslie & Christine Harris
Robert Edward Henderson
Peter John Heard
Mr. A. Hedges
Richard & Iris Holborow
Albert Edward Hazell
Emmeline Louise Hine
Jack P. Harrison
Maud A. Hicks
Emma Louise Hewitson
B. A. Humphries
Lomond Handley
Lucy Angelena Hooper
Mrs. J. Hodges
Michael & Barbara Hopkins
Ann Margaret Halls
Mr. E. D. Hawker
Peter A. D. Hyde
Gary D. Hawes
R. Hill
J. D. P. Hollingsworth
Barry & Josephine Henwood
Betty Kathleen Hedgcock
Pat Head
Lord Houghton
Alan & Maralyn Harvey
C. F. Hopkins
Mr. & Mrs. B. H. Irish
Harry Ingham
Hazel & Alan Jackson
Clare & David Jenkinson
Doreen Jones
K. P. A. Jackson
Lawrence R. D. Jenkins
Doris W. Jeffrey
Mr. & Mrs. Gordon Johnston
Ken James
Mr. & Mrs. D. G. Johnson
L. J. Janas
Simeon & Dawn James
Ken & John Jewell
Monica D. James
Trevor S. Jones
Olive May Johnson
Sheila & Norman James
Lucy & George Jenkinson
Jan Jones

Joy & Doug Keats
Joyce Kirby
Jenifer Annette Kinsey
Kay Kenrick
Jennifer Elizabeth Kendall
Dorothy Irene Kendall
David Knight
Elizabeth Knight
John Alfred Kent
Valerie Kemish
R. H. Lintott
Henry Stanley Lodwick
Edward George Lock
Valerie Ann Loveland
Frank J. Luery
Marjorie May Luscombe
Ann & Eric Lobb
Malcolm F. Lucas
Brian & Valerie Linford
Robert & Marie Linford
Andrew & Keith Linford
Jeanette V. Lee
Carolyn Lewis
Jimmy Lamb
Duncan Roy Luther
June & Michael Myers
May Marsh
Wendy Ann Martin
Jaqueline Marsh
Howard Matthew
Madge MacDonald
Rosemary Meyer
Eric Mowbray
Thomas A. Mills
Patricia Moore
Dale Marchi
Carole Anne Marchi
Douglas Martin
Hilda Mathews
Renee Miller
Ruby L. Mulley
Ted & Marion Marchant
David & Joyce Myers
Pamela Morris
Mrs. M. J. Metherell
Katherine Mowll
Pat & Joe Manning
Joyce Mary Massie
Suzanne Mens
Jame O'Donald Mays
Michele Suzanne Miles
Florence Ethel Maffey
Betty Margaret Morant
Mr. & Mrs. Charles Mudie
Anthony James Mines
John Martin
Brian Murray
Michael & Jane Macario
Doris Margaret Melbourne
Sarah Ann Milne
Michael McAleer
Patricia M. Mathews
Pamela & Alan Mills
Hilda Mabel Alice Milford
Alan & Mary Moncreaff
Michael & Betty McGrady
Richard Moore
Walter John Martin
James 'Fred' McKee
Jan Marsden
Graham & Linda Nolan
Mr. & Mrs. F. Neate

Mary Rose Norris
Jill Nield
Sophie Emma New
J. D. Netherall
Mr. S. A. Ormrod R.S.P.C.A.
Jo Orritt
Lindsay Oliver
Alan John O'Bland
Joseph Benedict Olverson
Alice Cheyne Ormanroyd
Valerie Oakley
Peter J. Purchase
C. & Mrs. P. Pickersgill
Beryl Jean Pearce
Ken & Enid Palmer
Edna Florence May Pike
Mr. & Mrs. A. Pike
Ruth & Lionel Parker
Gordon Perry
Tim & Ann Parker
Geoff & Joan Palmer
Hugh Nigel Patterson
Marie Eileen Pike
Mr. & Mrs. Ron Pope
Reginald & Elizabeth Page
Marie & Eric Poole
Dennis Penfold
Alma Pole
Jocelyn Purdy
Michael & Joyce Phelps
Robert Frank Pickett
Barbara Mary Pickering
Dr. & Mrs. A. Desmond Poole
Valerie Anne Pitt
H. Pasley
Doria Pettifer
Poulner Junior School
Robin Pelling
Phyllis Remfry
Yvonne Reed
Mrs. C. M. Rose
Antonia Ruffell
David Obrey Richards
John Robert Richards
Alan James Raphael
Desmond & Irene Redgrave
Lisa & David Richens
Christine Margaret Roberts
Dr. Donald James Roberts
Dr. Jonathon Mark Roberts
Elizabeth Anne Roberts
Elizabeth Robson
Alan & Ruth Redman
Derek & Sue Ruffell
Don & Diana Ruffell
Jack & Brenda Randall
Rick Richards
Claire Robertson
Dorothy Joy Reynolds
Betty & Ron Rutter
Angela & Robert Rutter
Gillian & Kenneth Rose
Angela Rushton
Margaret W. I. Russell
I. K. Ruck
Irene Rivett
Reg & Kay Redfearn
Ringwood Bookshop
Len & Anne Ruffell
Graham & Lynne Sirl
Louise Smee
Anne Saunders

Richard & Valerie Speake
Darrel & Carol Speake
Gayla Speake
Miriam & Dick Speake
Cresta Speake
Susan Patricia Smith
Geoff & Pauline Storer
W. H. Stanbury
Barbara & Gordon Scott
John Street
Jacqueline Anne Shone
Susan Patricia Spicer
Alan Sellwood
Peter & Maureen Soars
Arthur Alfred Staples
Eric Harold Stubbings
Frank Sutton
Herbert & Thelma Snudden
Ron & Norah Sims
Mr. A. Shilton
Marjorie Shaw
Brian & Anne Strong
Cyril Robert Smith
Christine & Tony Sanders
Mr. & Mrs. L. J. Stacey

Leslie & Brenda Skilton
Olive Maud Sutton-Smith
Mrs. J. E. Stewart
Marie Rose Steele
Enid M. Sage
Valerie L. Scott
Betty Lucy Stallard
Ronald A. Silverton
Steven & Chris Saunders
Thomas & Sylvia Shore
Steve Smith
Maureen Scurlock
Major C. G. Tuersley
Carla & Tony Tysoe
Pearl Tilley
Graham Trott
Peter & Hazel Tunbridge
Joan Thompson
Betty Doreen Thompson
David John Terry
M. I. Thorne
Betty Marion Taylor
Yvonne & Eric Thomas
Joyce E. Tofield
Elsie Thomas

Christopher Arthur Taylor
Dorothy Taylor
S. Tinsley
Marjorie & George Thorn
Bernard Taylor
Barbara Jane Thomas
Jackie Upward
Dr. Richard Vereker
Mel Voller
Stephen Valentine
Louis Valquier
George Clifford & Edith Walker
Jennifer Wills
Henry Woodward — *Artist*
Ted & Margi Whitlock
Joan Whitfield
Barbara White
Barrie Charles Wheatley
Richard & Jean Whitfield
Patricia & Liz Whittle
David Willis
Henry John Ashness Wells
Vera Kathleen West
Christine Willmott
Enid White

Dave & Sheila Whitehorn
Rosemary & George White
Kit Whitfield
Ann Jennifer Wyllie
R. A. Wallace
Shirley Victoria Waller
Derek John Williams
John & Betty Whicker
Stanley Waddington
Robert Whitlock
Cynthia Wood
G. R. & E. C. Wheeler
Gail Woffenden
Nora Williams-Jones
Brian 'Tich' & Pam Ward
Mike Watkins
Audrey Williams
Heather White
Sylvia Wilmott
Doris Mary Williams
Wessex Pictures
Joseé C. J. Faiure-Utteridge
A. A. Yale
Len & Jo Younger

My final thanks must go to David Small and his Staff at Brown & Son of Ringwood (including Jim Jones whose idea it was in the first place).

David has nurtured this project from embryo to adulthood. Through sleepless nights and worrying days he has designed, arranged and re-arranged the whole layout. It is due to his sensitive handling of my work that the visual affect of this book is so different and so pleasing. And I am proud to say that my book has been designed, printed and published by people local to the New Forest.

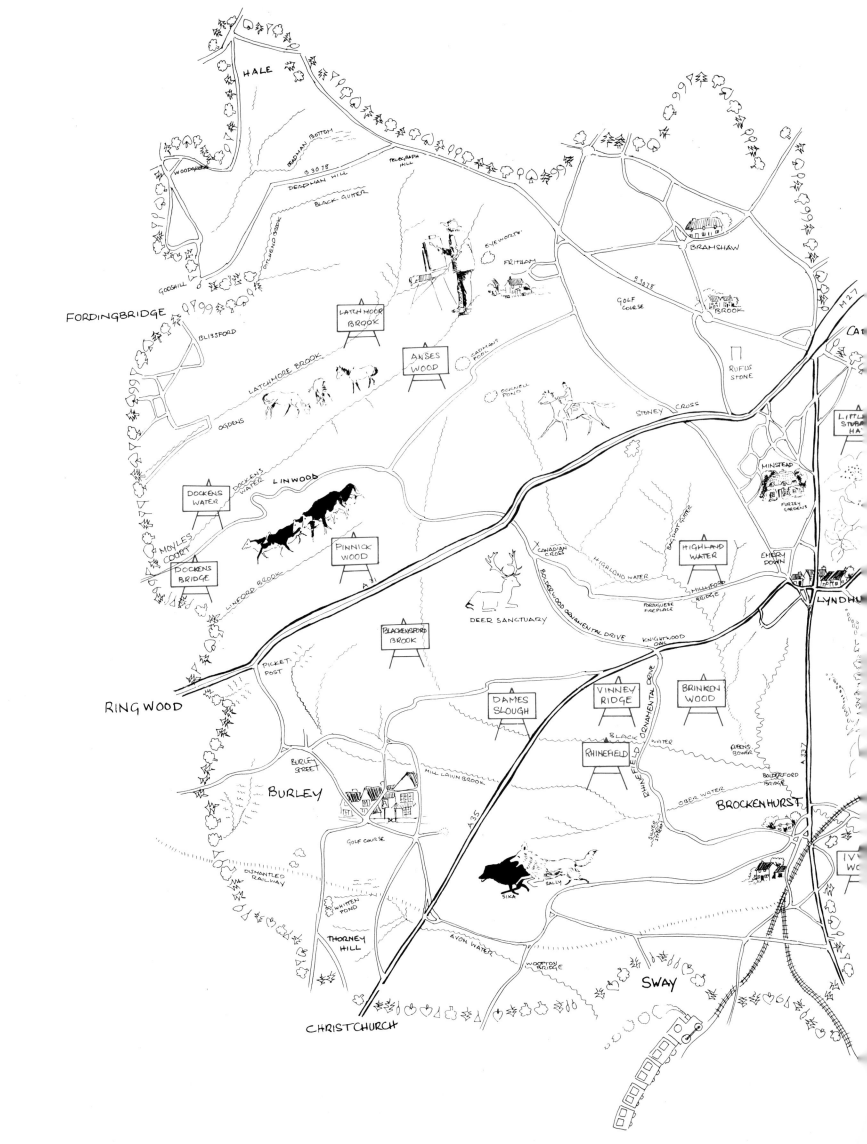

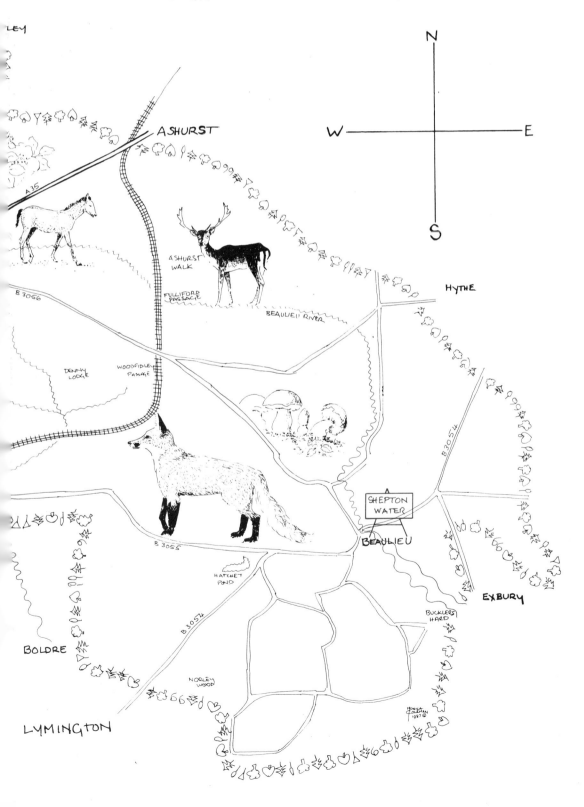

I believe that life is a series of tests. And everyone has their own cross to bear. Some people have more crosses than others. Some are tested more. My New Forest does have many cruel sides but it is one that is inflicted by mankind that is a cross of mine and I am constantly tested on how I carry it.

When you are weary from bearing yours, take your body into this place of nature. Let your mind be filled with the sounds and sights of wild things in their natural habitat, undisturbed by human interference. There is nothing more wonderful than to watch a fawn suckling its mother or to hear a fallow buck snorting during the rutting season. The rasping song of a Dartford warbler. Badger cubs romping at dusk. Fox cubs playing on a sunny afternoon. The curlews calling in spring. To walk through one of the Forest's old woods on a quiet, dull winter's day and suddenly be surrounded by a mass of small birds moving through feeding together. Chattering like a crowd of excited kids at the seaside. Blue tits, coal tits, great tits, tree creepers and nut-hatches.

If you enjoy my New Forest without causing any pain or disfigurement, then gradually your soul will open and absorb the beauty around you. Your cross will lighten and you will learn to pass the tests you are set.

ADDER

ROE BUCK.

SAND
LIZARD

VIXEN RESTING